Enchantment of the World

PARAGUAY

By Marion Morrison

Consultant for Paraguay: George I. Blanksten, Ph.D., Professor Emeritus of Political Science, Northwestern University, Evanston, Illinois

Consultant for Reading: Robert L. Hillerich, Ph.D., Professor Emeritus, Bowling Green State University; Consultant, Pinellas County Schools, Florida

CHILDRENS PRESS®
CHICAGO

City boys examine a new bicycle

Project Editor: Mary Reidy
Design: Margrit Fiddle

Library of Congress Cataloging-in-Publication Data

Morrison, Marion.
    Paraguay / by Marion Morrison.
        p.   cm. — (Enchantment of the world)
    Includes index.
    Summary: Introduces the geography, history,
agriculture, industry, and people of the South American
country known as "the place with the great river."
    ISBN 0-516-02619-4
    1. Paraguay—Juvenile literature. [1. Paraguay.]
I. Title. II. Series.
F2688.5.M67   1993
989.2—dc20   93-754
                                                    CIP
                                                    AC

Picture Acknowledgments
The Bettmann Archive: 29, 40, 43
© **Victor Englebert:** 57, 68 (2 photos), 71 (right), 103
North Wind Picture Archives: 27
Chip and Rosa Maria de la Cueva Peterson: 4, 8, 11, 63, 70
(2 photos), 73, 74, 76, 77, 83, 86 (2 photos), 89 (top), 90
(right), 111
Photri: 30, 78; © **ABY,** 12 (top)
Reuters/Bettmann: 54, 55
Root Resources: © **Wallace Murray,** 15; © **Piburn,** 56, 67
(top left), 93, 94 (left)
South American Pictures: © **Tony Morrison,** Cover,
Cover Inset, 10, 12 (center & bottom), 14, 16, 18 (center),
19 (left & right), 21 (left), 22 (2 photos), 33, 38, 58
(4 photos), 60, 64, 67 (right & bottom left), 71 (left), 72
(2 photos), 75, 79, 80, 82 (2 photos), 84, 85, 89 (bottom), 90
(left), 91 (2 photos), 94 (right), 97, 98, 99, 104, 107, 108, 110
(left); © **Marion Morrison,** 18 (right)
Travel Stock: © **Buddy Mays,** 5, 6, 20 (right), 23 (bottom
left), 31, 110 (right)
UPI/Bettmann: 47, 48 (2 photos), 49, 50 (2 photos), 52, 53
Valan: © **Jean-Marie Jro,** 18 (left); © **John Cancalosi,** 19
(center), 21 (right); © **Jim Merli,** 20 (left); © **Rob &
Melissa Simpson,** 23 (top left); © **Michel Bourque,** 23
(right); © **J.M. Giraud,** 100; © **Wouterloot-Gregoire,** 105
Len W. Meents: Maps on 69, 75
**Courtesy Flag Research Center, Winchester,
Massachusetts 01890:** Flag on back cover
Cover: Asunción—View across Plaza Independencia to
Legislative Palace and shanties
Cover Inset: Nanduti spiderweb lace, a traditional craft

These girls live in a small riverside village.

TABLE OF CONTENTS

Chapter 1

THE WORLD IN VIEW:
PARAGUAY

The small, landlocked republic of Paraguay lies almost in the heart of South America. It shares borders to the east, south, and west with the continent's two largest countries, Brazil and Argentina, and to the north with Bolivia, the only other country in South America without a coastline.

Paraguay's good river network, connecting with the Río de la Plata in Argentina, gives the country access to the Atlantic coast. The many rivers are probably responsible for the country's name, though the exact meaning of "Paraguay" is uncertain. It originates from the language of the Guaraní Indians and may mean "the place with the great river." A more complicated interpretation is "a river that is variously crowned" because of the floating islands of water hyacinths that "crown" the Río Paraguay when it is flooded.

The Guaraní were the largest group of Indians occupying the land that is now Paraguay when the Spaniards first arrived in the sixteenth century. Despite four hundred years of colonization by the Europeans, Guaraní language and culture have survived to this day. The country's currency is named the guaraní.

Paraguay had no rich silver or gold mines, but the explorers used the Río (river) Paraguay, hoping it would lead them to the

Opposite page: Water hyacinths form floating islands on the Río Paraguay

An abandoned Jesuit mission

rich Andean mines. When Spaniards eventually settled in the land of Paraguay, they found the Guaraní friendly and the land good for farming. Until they were expelled in 1767, Jesuit missionaries played an important role in the colony. Mostly life in colonial Paraguay was tranquil, compared with many other regions of South America.

Since the early nineteenth century when Paraguay became a republic, the country has experienced considerable strife. There have been disastrous conflicts with all of its neighbors, even including the small republic of Uruguay, which have resulted in the devastation of both the population and the economy. Dictatorship had been the most common form of government, but it ended when President Stroessner was ousted in 1989.

There are economic and political problems, but the Paraguayans are enjoying their newfound freedom and are looking forward to a more prosperous and brighter future.

Chapter 2

THE LAND

Paraguay, with an area of 157,048 square miles (406,755 square kilometers), is one of the smallest South American countries. It is surrounded by rivers that make up four-fifths of its borders. The Río Paraguay divides the country into two parts.

East of the Río Paraguay is the fertile, cultivated plateau where most of the 4.3 million people live, one-quarter of them in the metropolitan area of the capital, Asunción. To the west lies the Chaco, an inhospitable wilderness that covers almost 60 percent of the country and extends to within 60 miles (97 kilometers) of the foothills of the Andes mountains. The Chaco is very sparsely populated with less than 5 percent of the population. In places it is still barely explored.

THE RIVERS

The great rivers between Paraguay and her neighbors create natural frontiers. The Paraná, one of the major rivers of the continent, rises in the highlands of southern Brazil. It is 2,450 miles (3,943 kilometers) long, and empties into the Río de la Plata

The Río Paraná, with Argentina on the opposite shore

estuary. For 428 miles (689 kilometers) of its course it forms the borders between Paraguay and Brazil and between Paraguay and Argentina. At a point close to where the three countries meet are the Iguassú Falls, at one time part of Paraguay and now on the border between Argentina and Brazil.

The section between Paraguay and Brazil once held the record for the world's largest falls in volume of water, with seven times the volume of Niagara. The Guaíra Falls with hundreds of islands and torrents took the entire Río Paraná through a narrow gorge, until in 1982, Itaipú, the world's largest hydroelectric dam, was completed. Within forty days the gorge filled, a lake was created, and the falls were submerged.

Below the dam the Río Paraná continues in a southwesterly direction for 200 miles (322 kilometers) before turning west near the city of Encarnación, where another dam is being built. Farther downstream it is joined by its major tributary, the Río Paraguay.

The Paraguay is 1,584 miles (2,549 kilometers) long and the
fifth-largest river in South America. It rises in the Mato Grosso in
Brazil and in its upper course also forms part of the border
between Paraguay and Brazil. Flowing almost directly south, it
cuts through Paraguay dividing east from west, then forms the
frontier between Paraguay and Argentina for 150 miles (241
kilometers) before entering the Paraná.

For many years the principal route to and from the Atlantic
Ocean has been along the Paraná and Paraguay rivers. At one
time small oceangoing cargo vessels frequently made the journey
from Europe to Asunción. Except in the dry season, it is possible
to reach Concepción, upriver from Asunción, in small craft.

From the west, beginning among the snowy heights of the
Andes mountains, the Río Pilcomayo, 1,000 miles (1,609
kilometers) long, follows a shallow course across the Chaco
between Argentina and Paraguay and empties into the Río

Above: The second-largest city is Ciudad del Este.
Left: Ciudad del Este's leather market
Below: To build Highway 6, the highway between Ciudad del Este and Encarnación, forestland had to be destroyed.

Paraguay opposite Asunción. Pilcomayo comes from two Indian words meaning "red river," a name given long ago because of the russet earth washed down from the mountains during flood times.

The major rivers have many tributaries; one of these, the Río Apá, forms part of the northern borders of the country in the region of Concepción, where it flows into the Río Paraguay. The largest lake in Paraguay, the Ypoa, is at the edge of a swampy area close to the Río Paraguay and is connected to it by channels. Lake Ypacaraí, 21 miles (34 kilometers) east of Asunción, covers an area about 46 square miles (119 square kilometers) and drains into the Río Paraguay by a small river, the Salado. The lake is only 10 feet (3 meters) deep and has become a vacation center for people from the capital.

EAST OF THE RÍO PARAGUAY

Much of the land in this region is covered with rich alluvial soil. It is Paraguay's most fertile area. There is intense cultivation close to Asunción and in the area near Itaipú Dam and along the borders with Argentina and Brazil. Since the 1940s large tracts of forest have been cut down to make way for fields and grazing for cattle. More than 12 million acres (4,856,280 hectares) of forest have already been lost and the destruction is continuing. The change to the countryside is most obvious along the main roads linking the principal towns with the capital.

Highway 7 eastward to Ciudad del Este, Paraguay's second city, and the Río Paraná pass through rolling open country with well-cultivated fields. Ciudad del Este was previously called Puerto Presidente Stroessner. Highway 6, between the southern city of Encarnación and the east central region, cuts through land where

Charred skeletal remains of a once-luxuriant forest

forest destruction is in full swing. In many places the blackened or bleached skeletal trunks of immense trees stand as the only reminders of the original natural vegetation.

Many parts of southeastern Paraguay have small colonies of people of European origin. They keep their small villages and settlements in their own traditional style. Their orchards and farms and long carts drawn by horses could be part of Eastern Europe. Surrounded by orange trees, the small town of Villarrica has many German colonists and is the center of a rich farming area.

Villages like Itauguá near Asunción have grown from their Spanish origins. Low whitewashed buildings with colonnades and tile roofs surround grassy plazas. They have large churches that

A panoramic view of the Chaco

once were the focal point, and the towns around them have developed with dirt or cobbled streets.

To the northeast along the border with Brazil the land is broken by low, rounded, forested hills that are extensions of the Brazilian plateau. The Cordillera (mountains) de Amambay and Cordillera de Mbaracayú are composed of crystalline rocks and sandstones and reach their highest point at Ponta Porá at just over 2,000 feet (610 meters).

Another range with various names, known in Paraguay as the Cordillera of Caaguazú, extends southwest toward the center of this region. The San Rafael peak, the highest point, is 2,789 feet (850 meters).

In the north Concepción and Pedro Juan Caballero are the two most important towns, though still quite isolated as the road network linking them is largely unpaved.

THE CHACO

The Chaco covers 95,350 square miles (246,957 square kilometers) and is almost the size of the state of Oregon. It is a

Cattle grazing on the "low" Chaco

level, virtually featureless land, and the principal access is by the Trans-Chaco Highway from Asunción. The largest town is Villa Hayes, while Filadelfia, 290 miles (467 kilometers) northwest of Asunción, is the center of a colony of Mennonite immigrants who arrived early in the twentieth century. Mariscal Estigarribia, farther north and west, is a small town and military outpost.

The Chaco is divided into two types of land identified by vegetation and rainfall. The "low" Chaco between the Paraguay and Pilcomayo rivers, in the south, is swampy. Palms and forests may be inundated by floodwater, depending on the season and the amount of rain. Pastures and savanna between the palms are used for cattle ranching, and large *estancias*, "cattle ranches," have been established. Some, many miles from the highway, are reached only by light aircraft.

Away from the rivers and to the northwest, the "high" Chaco has little rainfall and an average daily temperature of 90 degrees Fahrenheit (32 degrees Celsius), although it is often hotter. Much of the vegetation of the high Chaco is spiny, scrub forest interspersed with cactus. Cattle roam this inhospitable region and are rounded up by herders who wear leather covers to protect their arms and legs. In some parts where the land is less arid, the forest contains a mixture of hardwoods, including *quebracho*, "the ax breaker."

CLIMATE

Paraguay enjoys a subtropical climate with few extremes of temperature. The summer months are generally warm with the daytime average in Asunción reaching 78 degrees Fahrenheit (26 degrees Celsius). The winter months of June and July are slightly cooler and in the south the daily average temperature may reach 50 degrees Fahrenheit (10 degrees Celsius). Snow is unknown, but in the open fields frost can occur.

During an average year some rain falls throughout the country in each month. Rainfall is greatest in the north and east and gradually decreases to a minimum of about 30 inches (76 centimeters) in the Chaco, where the driest months are July, August, and September. Some years there are droughts that are often followed by heavy rain and serious flooding. June 1983 will be remembered for some of the worst flooding of the Río Paraguay, when it rose 15 feet (4.5 meters) above normal at Asunción, drenching many riverside communities.

FLORA

It is hardly surprising that the national tree of Paraguay is the lapacho, which flowers abundantly in July and August. Yellow-

Some of the trees found in Paraguay are the palo borracho *or "drunken tree" (far left), pink-flowered lepachos (left), and palm trees (above).*

flowered and pink-flowered lapachos make a show of brilliant color through the woodlands, parks, and roadsides.

The humid forests of eastern Paraguay that have survived are similar to rain forests, with many tall trees, including hardwoods such as the acacia and the cedrela. Bromeliads, a variety of mosses and ferns, are packed together and are often difficult to penetrate. Some areas have been set aside as reserves, such as the Mbaracayú Forest in the cordillera of the same name.

A different vegetation covers the Chaco. In the low flooded areas palms are abundant and the pools are covered with floating plants including lilac-colored water hyacinths. In the higher places a scrub of spiny bushes and low trees include the *palo borracho*, "drunken tree," with its strangely bulbous trunk that is an adaptation to conserve water. Near the rivers the scrub vegetation gives way to clusters of trees, of which the quebracho is the best known.

The rhea, a flightless bird that resembles an ostrich, is Paraguay's largest bird (far left). Wood storks (left) live in swampy regions and toucans (above) live in forested areas.

BIRDS

The largest bird of Paraguay is the rhea. It resembles the ostrich and is a flightless species of the grasslands and open places. An adult averages 5 feet (1.5 meters) in height. These grayish-brown birds live in flocks of up to thirty-eight individuals.

Among the smallest birds are many species of hummingbirds, which are seen in all parts of the country. The swampy regions and river edges provide the habitat for many water birds, among them herons, egrets, the wood stork, and the maguari stork. The larger jabiru stork is common, especially in isolated areas.

A totally different variety of bird exists in the forested places where other food is available. Fruit-eating birds such as toucans with their ungainly and colorful bills can be recognized by their bobbing flight as they cross open spaces. The many parrots, parakeets, and macaws also eat fruit and nuts, and some of these

Above: A young boy holds a caiman whose mouth is held shut for the boy's protection. Anacondas (top left) can still be found in swampy areas.

birds are well known locally. No one can miss the huge, unkempt, communal nest of twigs built by the monk parakeet.

The most familiar birds of the dry woodlands include the ovenbirds, which build immense dome-shaped nests. Locally they are called *horneros*, Spanish for the clay ovens still used in rural areas. Of the same family are the firewood gatherers, small inconspicuous birds that build massive nests of twigs.

FAUNA

The fauna is rich and varied. In the large areas of swamp and river that occur in every part of the country crocodilians such as the jacare or caiman were once abundant, but hunting has severely depleted the population. In some of the swamps the

The capybara (above), the world's largest rodent, is semiaquatic. The agouti (top left), another rodent, is rabbit sized and lives in the forest.

anaconda, or water boa, is still found. The anaconda is a constrictor snake that crushes its prey. It may grow to a length of 25 feet (7.6 meters) and perhaps more. Poisonous snakes belong to the family of pit vipers, which include rattlesnakes and the fer-de-lance.

In some of the swamps large semiaquatic capybara are common. Capybara are about the size of a pig and are the world's largest rodent. They are equally at home in water, forest, or in grassland where they usually move about in family groups.

Typical of the forest are the peccaries, similar to wild pigs. Other forest dwellers include tiny brocket deer and many different rodents, including rabbit-sized agoutis and the slightly larger pacas that keep to the forest floor.

Various monkeys including the black howler monkey and the capuchin monkey remain in parts of the Chaco. Armadillos too

Two kinds of armadillos are the banded armadillo (left) and the fairy armadillo (right).

are common, including, in sandy places, the smallest of all armadillos, the *pichy ciego* or "blind pichy."

While the list of wildlife is apparently endless, the myriads of insects must not be forgotten. Butterflies mass by the thousands in damp, slightly salty places, and drivers crossing the Chaco remark on the clouds of insects meeting their vehicles like gentle rain.

FISH

An abundance of fish can be found in the rivers and lagoons. One scientific expedition to the Río Pilcomayo collected seventy-five species, among them curiosities such as the lungfish. This fish makes a cocoon in the bottom of the mud. When the water evaporates completely during a drought, the lungfish breathes air through a small hole in the mud.

Of the better-known fish seen in markets, some like the dorado can weigh about 15 pounds (6.8 kilograms), and there are huge catfish. Apart from these species there are piranhas, the voracious

A giant blue Morpho butterfly, covered with dewdrops (left), and the owl butterfly (top left); many fish are found in the rivers and lagoons. The piranha (above) has razor-sharp teeth.

so-called attack fish with razor-sharp teeth. Forest-dwelling Indians at one time used piranha teeth for cutting their hair and trimming arrows. Although the piranha can be dangerous if there is blood in the water, a ray that is common in shallow places also can hurt bathers with its sharp dorsal spine by inflicting a painful wound that if untreated soon turns gangrenous.

NATURAL RESOURCES

Paraguay has few natural mineral resources and there is little mining activity. Small deposits of uranium, bauxite, iron ore, manganese, and copper are known, but none of these appear to be economic to work, as they are not easily accessible and transportation is difficult. Oil exploration has yet to reveal anything substantial.

The country's greatest resource has been the fertile soil of east Paraguay and the pastures in the Chaco. The soil enables the population to feed itself effectively, and the pastures are the basis of the cattle ranching industry, which until recently was an important factor in the export market. The need to cultivate cash crops such as soybeans and cotton is now threatening another rich resource—the forests—where there are hardwoods and a variety of other useful timbers.

In the past twenty years Paraguay has begun to tap its rich natural resource, the rivers. Surrounded by so much water, the possibilities for hydroelectric energy are infinitely greater than the country will ever need. At present wood is still the primary source of fuel in Paraguay, but this will change once electricity is installed across the country. Then not only can this energy be harnessed to create a sound industrial base in Paraguay but there will be an enormous surplus for sale to neighboring countries.

Fish are an untapped resource because the people, as in so many South American countries, have always preferred to eat meat.

POTENTIAL

Since gaining its independence from Spain early in the nineteenth century, Paraguay has had little chance to develop its potential. With a succession of leaders and governments that have subjected the country to periods of extreme isolation, devastating war, or dictatorship, it is only now, in the 1990s, that the republic has a real opportunity to work toward social and industrial improvement. This has been made possible by the promise of democratic elections and the economic stability that the Itaipú Dam and other similar projects should ensure.

Chapter 3
HISTORY TO
INDEPENDENCE

THE GUARANÍ INDIANS

The largest group of people inhabiting the land of Paraguay at the time the Europeans arrived was the Guaraní-speaking Indians. Other groups, with their own language, included the Caingang and the Guayakí. All were descendants of the first inhabitants of the Americas who some ten thousand to twenty thousand years earlier had made their way across the Bering Strait to Alaska to spread through the American continents.

By the time of the Spanish conquest in the early sixteenth century, the Guaraní had developed from being hunter gatherers to seminomadic farmers. They were accomplished plant growers, although still supplementing their diets with fruits from the forest and fish from the rivers. In the traditional manner of many Indian tribes, the Guaraní cleared patches of forest by the slash-and-burn method, using the area for a short time and moving on when the soil became exhausted. The cleared areas were shared by communities of Guaraní cultivating a variety of crops, including manioc and maize (corn), the main staple foods, and beans, potatoes, bananas, and papayas. The Guaraní looked to the stars to tell them when to plant and sow, and they had only a digging stick as their main agricultural tool.

The Guaraní lived communally in a village, sharing a few very large houses ranged around a square plaza. If protection from other tribes was necessary, stockades and moats were built around the village. Some of the houses were more than 150 feet (46 meters) long, and natural plants such as grass and palm leaves were used as thatch. On the inside the houses were divided to accommodate each family, and sometimes as many as sixty families lived under the same roof.

Household items included small pottery dishes and bowls and large jars in which the Indians stored a strong beerlike brew made from maize. Large jars also were used as funerary urns, as it was the custom among the Guaraní to bury their dead in jars in the ground, and examples of these have been found by archaeologists.

Hammocks were woven of cotton or made from palm fibers, and cotton woven into cloth was worn occasionally as a covering by the women. For personal decoration, the Guaraní liked to paint their bodies in patterns of dots and stripes with natural dyes from the forest. The men wore huge shell necklaces or occasionally silver or copper chest pendants. Most distinctive was the T-shaped stick worn as a lip ornament.

The Guaraní community affairs were directed by a council of chiefs, a position in which a father was often succeeded by his son. But the real power lay with the village *shaman*, who was a priest believed to possess supernatural powers. The Guaraní practiced cannibalism, but it seems they treated their victims with great respect. A prisoner might be kept for months, or maybe years, was given a wife, could boast of his own achievements and

An old lithograph shows Indians who once lived on the banks of the Río Paraná.

those of his tribe, and was allowed to throw stones at his captors. When the time came, however, he was ceremoniously sacrificed in the main plaza. Children of the tribe were encouraged to crush the victim's skull and perform certain rituals to ensure they became strong warriors. The Guaraní used the long bones of their victims and enemies to make flutes.

The original homelands of the Guaraní were in the east between the Paraguay and Paraná rivers, but they extended their territory east into what is now Brazil, south into the estuary of the Río de la Plata, and west into the Chaco, where they subdued the hostile native tribes. By the end of the fifteenth century, groups of Guaraní had made incursions into the land of the powerful Incas, whose Andean empire extended from the present-day country of Ecuador through Peru and Bolivia and into northern Chile.

Some of the Guaraní settled in Inca territory, but others returned to their native land with gold and silver, metals that were abundant in Inca mines and rivers but were not found in

Guaraní territory. It was the sight of these precious metals that enticed Spanish explorers arriving in the Río de la Plata, or River of Silver, as it is known in Spanish, to venture upriver and cross the unknown continent in search of the legendary wealth of El Dorado.

SPANISH SAILOR EXPLORERS

Christopher Columbus reconnoitered part of the South and Central American coastlines for the first time on his third and fourth voyages. This led the way for the many large and small expeditions that subsequently set sail from Europe at the beginning of the sixteenth century in the "age of discovery." Many sailor explorers were intent, as Columbus was, on finding a route to the Indies and the Spice Islands, but instead found themselves in the New World.

The sailors who arrived off the east coast of South America were astonished by the size of the river estuaries, particularly that of the Amazon in northern Brazil, which they named "The Sweet Sea." The other, the Río de la Plata, is an estuary formed by the Paraná and Uruguay rivers. It is not as large as the Amazon but it is equally awesome. The first recorded Spanish expedition to enter the Río de la Plata in 1516 was led by Juan Días de Solís. He too was searching for a route to the Indies and no doubt thought the river was a strait that would lead him to his destination. His hopes were short-lived, however, as he and some of his companions were ambushed by Indians and killed.

Some of the sailors who escaped, however, had seen the silver and gold of the Indians and realized they were on the right track in their search for riches. This was confirmed by the explorer

Aleixo García. He and a few others became the first white men to sail up the Río Paraguay where he joined the Guaraní in a raid on the Incas. He sent word of his findings to the renowned navigator, Sebastian Cabot, who had arrived off the Brazilian coast in 1526. García said he had spoken with Indians who "wore silver crowns on their heads and gold plates hanging from their necks and ears and attached around their belts."

This message was enough to make Cabot alter the course of his journey and head upriver into the Río Paraguay. His expedition, however, was a failure. There was quarreling among the men, who, weakened by a lack of food, failed to reach the land of the Incas. But again enough information had been collected to spur the next expedition, one of the biggest to leave Spain for the New World in the sixteenth century. It was led by Pedro de Mendoza and included eleven ships, more than a thousand men, a hundred horses, pigs, and "horned cattle." This expedition reached the land of the Incas. Mendoza successfully collected some twenty loads of gold and silver; but, on his return he, too, and some of his companions were massacred by Indians.

Juan de Salazar,
the founder of Asunción

Mendoza did, however, leave a lasting memorial to his efforts. The Spanish Emperor Charles V had decreed that a settlement be established in the area as a base for future expeditions. A first attempt to create such a settlement in the Río de la Plata was on the site of present-day Buenos Aires. The settlement failed because of the hostility of the local Pampa Indians. Instead Mendoza sent some of his men upriver to search for a suitable place to found a small fort. One of his commanders, Juan de Salazar, chose a bluff on the Río Paraguay. In 1537 a small wooden fort was established and named Nuestra Señora de la Asunción, which in due course developed to become the capital city of Paraguay.

For about forty years Asunción was the headquarters of all Spanish possessions in southern South America, until 1580 when Buenos Aires was finally and successfully refounded. The Europeans and Indians got along well together. The Guaraní were friendly, provided food for the Spaniards, and were eager to join them as allies in their campaigns. They did not object to the

Mestizo children

foreigners mixing with their women, whose native beauty was a
great attraction. From these early associations grew the first
mestizo, or mixed Spanish and Indian, population in the region.

It was not long, however, before the Indians became subject to
exploitation by the foreigners. The system known as the
encomienda was introduced in the middle of the sixteenth century.
Many Spaniards, having given up the struggle to find great
mineral riches, took over the best of the land and settled into
farming and cattle raising. Under the encomienda, Spanish
landowners could organize groups of Indians into forced labor in
return for teaching them a Christian way of life. In reality the
Indians were often mistreated and thousands died. Several
Guaraní leaders led revolts against their exploitation, but they
were not successful. The number of Indians declined further as the
mestizo population grew. By the end of the sixteenth century,
fewer than three thousand Indians remained within a twenty-one-
mile (thirty-four-kilometer) radius of Asunción.

At the beginning of the seventeenth century, Paraguay became a separate colony and Hernando Arias de Saavedra, known to everyone as Hernandarias, was appointed governor. He was the first *criollo* (person of Spanish blood born in the colonies) to hold such a position anywhere in Latin America.

THE JESUIT MISSIONS

Spanish explorers were accompanied by priests and missionaries intent on converting the native people to Christianity. In 1565 the first bishop arrived in Asunción followed shortly by three Jesuit missionaries. With the blessing of Governor Hernandarias, the first Jesuit mission was established in 1609. By the end of the sixteenth century, thirty missions, or *reductions*, housed more than 100,000 Guaraní. The missions spread over a large area of the Río de la Plata and into Bolivia and northern Chile, with about eight inside the boundaries of modern Paraguay.

The Guaraní were happy to be in the missions. They had been exploited by the encomienda and the settlers. They were an easy target for the dreaded *mamelucos*, the slave raiders from Brazil. Even the missions could not always protect the Indians from the slave raids. During the first half of the sixteenth century there were some fierce battles. Several of the reductions were burned down and thousands of Indians either killed or captured. The mamelucos were well organized with horses and arms and were backed by Indian supporters with blowpipes and poisoned arrows. The Jesuits and Guaraní had little more than bows and arrows or clubs with which to defend themselves.

The aim of the missions, however, was to offer much more than just protection. They were well-organized societies in which work

The Jesuits developed the artistic talents of the Guaraní Indians. This statue was carved by the Guaraní in the seventeenth century.

and responsibility were shared equally. At the same time care was taken not to disrupt the traditional framework of Indian society. Chiefs remained at the head of a number of families within the missions.

Much of the work was agricultural. The Indians grew maize, manioc, sugarcane, and fruit. Many of the missions also kept thousands of head of cattle, and the Indians worked as herders and cowboys. Additionally some missions were commercially successful in exporting cotton, tobacco, hardwoods, and hides. Most important of all was *yerba maté*, a refreshing tea that was made from the leaves of a native plant.

When not working, the Indians were kept busy studying or developing their artistic talents. The missionaries found them to be willing pupils. Some were able to absorb a classical education, while others were particularly capable in the more practical arts of weaving, boat building, printing, and carpentry.

The missions provided the Indians with everything they needed to pursue their skills. There were libraries that housed hundreds of books and works of art and workshops equipped with imported tools of every kind.

The success of the missions caused a great deal of resentment. The settlers and the slave traders wanted to use the Indians as slave labor and objected to their being out of reach in the missions. Spanish landowners were envious of the Jesuit control of the highly profitable yerba maté trade. Other religious orders disliked the Jesuits. But most of all it was the wealth and power that the missions had amassed that caused the hostility. By organizing private armies to defend themselves against raiders, the Jesuits gave rise to rumors that they were creating "a state within a state." The rumors and accusations reached a level that could no longer be ignored by the Spanish crown. In 1767, more than 150 years after the Jesuits had arrived, they were expelled from all the Spanish colonies in South America.

It was a tragic decision for the Guaraní and other South American Indians. Not long after the Jesuits' departure, there was little to show for their efforts. The mission villages, built around central plazas with their churches on one side and Indian dwellings on the other, were raided and burned down. The beautiful paintings and carvings were stolen or destroyed and churches left in ruins. There was nothing left for the Indians who, if they escaped being forced into slave labor, returned once more to their primitive lives in the forest.

FROM COLONY TO INDEPENDENCE

During the four hundred years of colonial rule, the Spanish crown showed little interest in the small colony around the Río

Paraguay. In the beginning Asunción had been important as the base from which expeditions set out westward to Bolivia and east to Brazil. In 1580 Buenos Aires was in fact refounded by settlers traveling downriver from the small fort. But in 1617, when the Spanish crown, realizing the potential of the new settlement and port on the Río de la Plata, separated Buenos Aires from the province of Paraguay, Asunción was effectively forgotten.

Lack of intervention by the Spanish crown in the affairs of the colony helped to create a society rather different from that in other parts of Latin America. The mixed mestizo population continued to grow, but not at the expense of Indian tradition and culture, which remained very strong. From the beginning, though, there was considerable tension between the *peninsulares* (Spaniards born in Spain but living in the colonies) and the criollos. Many peninsulares held important posts in the bureaucracy, the church, and the military. The criollos were powerful landowners and men of authority who often had profitable commercial interests.

The criollos had a strong sense of independence. As early as 1721 they gave their support to an attempt to overthrow the Spanish governor. This was one of the most serious uprisings against Spanish authority anywhere on the continent up to that time. Disorder and unrest gave the Portuguese, who had colonies in Brazil, the opportunity to seize a large area of land in the north of the province, which has remained in Brazil ever since. Fear of losing territory to both Brazil and Argentina was a constant problem for the colony, which was forced to maintain an expensive and permanent defense system.

In 1776 the Paraguay province was made part of the Viceroyalty of La Plata, based in Buenos Aires. This decision came at much the same time that Spain was changing what had been long-standing restrictive regulations on trade. Trading was permitted through a few specific ports in Spain and the colonies, although in practice the authorities could never control the contraband goods that passed through other ports. Once the colonies were legally allowed to trade in a wider market, commerce boomed. In the Río de la Plata region Buenos Aires in particular became prosperous with a large increase in the export of hides to Europe. It was only a matter of time before the colonists, particularly the criollos, demanded still more trading freedom and release from payment of the taxes they had been obliged to make to Spain. Such thoughts were also encouraged by the flow of liberal ideas spreading from Europe, where the French Revolution had taken place at the end of the eighteenth century.

The majority of people in the colonies were still not sure they wanted total independence. But when in 1808 Napoleon Bonaparte of France invaded Spain, deposed the Spanish King Ferdinand VII, and instead installed Joseph Bonaparte, revolutionaries chose that moment to remove some of the Spanish authorities in the colonies. In Argentina the criollos of Buenos Aires deposed their viceroy in 1810. They called on the people of Asunción to take similar action with their governor. When the Paraguayans refused, Argentina sent in a military force led by General Belgrano to make the Paraguayans change their mind. Belgrano was met with fierce opposition and forced to retreat. In the following year, however, Paraguayan patriots took the initiative. On their own they deposed the Spanish governor and, virtually without bloodshed or conflict, declared independence.

Chapter 4

THE MODERN REPUBLIC

EL SUPREMO

After declaring independence Paraguay needed to ensure it was not absorbed by Argentina. A *junta*, a body of men, was appointed to govern the new republic. It was led by Fulgencio Yegros, the army captain responsible for deposing the Spanish governor. The junta was dominated by a civilian lawyer, Dr. José Gaspar Rodríguez de Francia. In 1811 Francia used his legal skills to negotiate a treaty with the authorities in Buenos Aires so that Argentina recognized Paraguay's independence.

When Argentina later called on Paraguay to assist it with military help, Francia refused. Buenos Aires tried to force the issue by blockading Paraguay, but Francia responded by calling together a new congress and formally declaring Paraguay independent on October 12, 1813. Francia refused to negotiate further treaties with Buenos Aires. A year later Francia was declared supreme dictator of the republic, even though there was no constitution or other form of authority to restrain his power. Initially he was to hold the position for five years, but in 1816 he was confirmed dictator for life.

*A statue of Dr. José Gaspar
Rodríguez de Francia*

"El Supremo," as Francia was called, was born in Paraguay,
where his father was a supervisor of a tobacco plantation. He
studied at the University of Cordoba in Argentina and became a
lawyer, taking every opportunity he could to defend the legal
rights of the Guaraní Indians to whom he was known as *Caraí*, or
"Great Chief." The Guaraní always remained Francia's greatest
supporters. Francia was a highly educated man, with a very
austere life-style. He held firm views and used all the means at his
disposal, including the army, police, and a sophisticated spy
network, to impose them. He ruled Paraguay with an iron will
until his death in 1840. He persecuted the Roman Catholic church
and the Spanish elite (regarded as a socially superior group). He
dissolved the monasteries, stripped the church of its property, and
did not allow it to play any part in the country's affairs. The
Spanish elite were deprived of their wealth and property and

forbidden to marry within their own circles. Francia decreed that only he could authorize marriages, although he never married. In 1820 El Supremo discovered a conspiracy to depose him in favor of the "Old Spaniards," who were then subjected to a vicious reign of terror. Hundreds of suspects were arrested and tortured and many were executed, including Francia's old associate Yegros.

Some justification for Francia's attitude to the elite and the church was his belief that they exploited the poor, the working classes, and the Indians. Despite the fear and awe he inspired, the majority of the population supported him. In later years his power was so absolute that he ordered everyone to wear a hat, just so they could doff it in his presence. To disobey meant an immediate trip to prison. Perhaps the most extraordinary decision made by Francia was to seal the borders of Paraguay. No one was allowed to enter or depart, and all external trading was forbidden. This was retaliation against the early attempt by Buenos Aires to blockade the republic, but it also kept out foreign influence and liberal ideas that El Supremo felt might undermine his position.

As the republic needed to be self-sufficient, Francia assumed responsibility for agricultural planning and sought to resolve problems when they arose. He was remarkably successful, and the country produced occasional large crops of maize, wheat, peanuts, sweet potatoes, various other vegetables, sugarcane, cotton, tobacco, and maté. But even when there were surpluses that could be traded elsewhere for commercial profit, Francia refused to relax his isolationist policy. Perhaps he was right, because the republic did enjoy years of relative peace and prosperity while most other countries in South America were in a state of chaos following independence.

Carlos Antonio López

It was the death of Francia that produced the greatest threat of upheaval for Paraguay. The republic still had no constitution and El Supremo had made no arrangements for anyone to succeed him.

THE FATHER OF PARAGUAY

However, a leader did emerge without too much disruption. Carlos Antonio López governed at first as one of two consuls; the other was a military man. In 1844 a congress was convened. It ratified a constitution and elected López the first president of Paraguay.

Carlos Antonio López came from a modest background. He was one of eight children, and his father was a tailor. López was a lawyer and well known as an efficient and able administrator. It has been suggested that because he had political aspirations, López kept a low profile during Francia's dictatorship. An opposing theory holds that he was Francia's nephew, but there does not seem to be any evidence to support this.

Certainly Carlos Antonio López held some very different views from El Supremo. Without delay he opened Paraguay's borders to the outside world. Initially his plans were foiled by the dictator Juan Manuel de Rosas of Argentina, who closed the Río de la Plata to Paraguayan ships and trade, but this stopped with Rosas' death in 1852. López restored power to the Catholic church, reinstated the old Spanish families, released Francia's political prisoners, and in 1842 abolished slavery.

Carlos Antonio López was closer to El Supremo in his economic policies. Both men believed the land should belong to the state, to be rented out to families as required. Private ownership was discouraged, and under López it was illegal for foreigners to purchase land. Two of the most important crops, yerba maté and tobacco, continued to be state monopolies. López added a third—timber—which was an important natural resource, easily accessible in the extensive forests and potentially very valuable.

With only limited experience and knowledge, having been brought up inside the closed frontiers of Paraguay, President López recognized the need to modernize his country and directed his energies to this end. He welcomed, even persuaded, hundreds of foreign experts to work in Paraguay, including engineers, builders, mechanics, and surgeons. Education, transportation, and communication were priorities. During his dictatorship an estimated four hundred schools were built, scholarships were arranged for bright students to study abroad, the first newspaper was printed in 1845, and a telegraph line was started. The Río Paraguay was opened to steam navigation, the country's road system was developed, and the first railway was constructed, which was one of the first on the continent. With the building of medical clinics, a hospital service was started.

Carlos Antonio López was not as successful, however, in his foreign relations. There was still the fear that Argentina or Brazil might invade Paraguay, a fear that threatened to become a reality when in 1855 Brazil put a major naval expedition on the Río Paraná. To counter such threats, the president employed many foreign technicians on military projects such as iron foundries for making cannon and naval equipment, a large arsenal at Asunción, and a huge fortress overlooking the Río Paraguay, all of which he felt were essential for Paraguay's protection.

President López remained in power until his death in 1862. There were times during his dictatorship when he was ruthless, and he made himself the country's leading land and cattle owner. He must be credited, though, with laying the foundations of the modern state of Paraguay, and he is sometimes referred to as the "father" of the republic.

FRANCISCO SOLANO LÓPEZ

When Francisco Solano López succeeded his father, the people of Paraguay had every reason to look forward to a positive and prosperous future. The country was in many respects in advance of its neighbors. López was a young man, trained for the presidency, well educated, with a command of two or three European languages, who had already shown himself to be a capable soldier. Admittedly in his youth he had been spoiled and pampered, could be arrogant, and had an eye for the girls that often got him into trouble, but he always had been bailed out by his father.

*Francisco Solano López
succeeded his father as president.*

   By the age of eighteen López was a general and six years later
was appointed general-in-chief of the Paraguay army and minister
of war. Shortly after the appointment his father sent him on a
mission to Europe, to make contacts and acquire the expert help
and technical supplies Paraguay needed. He carried out his duties
efficiently and responsibly. He was received at the court of Queen
Isabella II of Spain and also by the king of the Two Sicilies in Italy.
He was particularly honored with the warm reception he received
in Paris from the Emperor Napoleon III and the Empress Eugenie.
Napoleon Bonaparte was his boyhood idol, and there is no doubt
that this meeting with Bonaparte's nephew had a profound effect
on López.
   Francisco Solano López's journey to Europe was also significant
because he met the lady who became his companion for life and
mother of his four children. Eliza Lynch came from an Irish
family that had become impoverished during the potato famine in

43

the 1840s. She was a woman of remarkable beauty, who had made her way into Parisian social circles following a disastrous marriage at the age of fifteen. Well qualified to assist with introductions and protocol, Eliza became Francisco's constant companion. She accompanied him back to Paraguay and received a hostile reception. Carlos Antonio López made it clear that she was not the woman he had in mind for his son, and while he was alive, the family never accorded Eliza the respect she might have hoped for.

Matters improved for Eliza once Francisco Solano López became president. She worked hard to introduce into Paraguayan society a touch of European artistry and culture. One of her favorite projects was the national theater. She was resented by members of the old society, but no one could question that in the troubled years to come, she remained Francisco's most ardent and loyal supporter.

It is doubtful that anyone could have foreseen the total devastation into which Paraguay was to be plunged over the next few years. Perhaps it might never have happened had López heeded his father's advice to try and resolve problems—especially with Brazil—"not with the sword, but with the pen."

THE WAR OF THE TRIPLE ALLIANCE

In 1864 Brazil invaded Uruguay, a small country that, like Paraguay, acts as a buffer between Brazil and Argentina. Brazil took this action to support one side in a civil war that was tearing Uruguay apart. In doing so Brazil ignored President López's warning not to intervene. As a result Marshal López, as he liked to be called, felt obliged to come to the aid of Uruguay.

López seized a Brazilian ship that was on the Río Paraguay, sent part of his army north to invade Brazil, and prepared to dispatch another section of the army into Uruguay. To get to Uruguay, the Paraguayan army had to cross Argentina. When it was refused permission, the marshal declared war on Argentina as well. Finally when Uruguay, under a puppet government, joined forces with Brazil and Argentina, Paraguay found itself ranged against all three countries in the War of the Triple Alliance.

Clearly the odds were stacked against Paraguay, which suffered severe losses almost immediately. The fleet was virtually destroyed in 1865. In 1866 López lost almost twenty thousand men, the cream of his army. López demanded, and got, great loyalty from his men, in particular from the Guaraní, who had always been courageous in battle. The marshal, though, also was capable of extreme cruelty and was known to have executed members of his own army who survived a lost battle. Eliza created her own army of women.

By 1869 the battle was virtually over. Pursued by the Alliance armies, President López retreated across the interior of Paraguay with his shattered forces, thousands of his countrymen suffering from disease and starvation. Driven by fear of conspiracy, and perhaps a little mad by this time, López committed an ultimate act of cruelty by executing many hundreds of his followers, including his own two brothers and other members of his family. Eliza, though, lived to witness his final defeat and death at the hands of Brazilian cavalrymen in a remote spot near the Brazilian border, where she buried him in a shallow grave.

The war had taken a horrendous toll. Almost half the population had died—including nine out of every ten men. Some of its territory was annexed and the republic was occupied by

Brazil and Argentine forces until 1876. Huge debts had accumulated and the country was devastated. It was the bloodiest war in Latin-American history.

RECOVERY AND THE CHACO WAR

In the aftermath of war, as order emerged from chaos, Paraguay's two main political parties were founded, the conservative *Colorado* or "Red" party and the Liberal or "Blue" party. The Colorados evolved from people associated with Marshal López and his heroic efforts. They held power for nearly thirty years until unseated by a Liberal revolt in 1904. The Liberal party was created by the intellectual and future president, Cecilio Báez, who put his writing skills to good use in spreading his political message.

The Liberals were no more successful than the Colorados in achieving political stability. There were ten presidents between 1904 and 1912, with four in 1911 alone. Some economic progress was made. Foreign experts and new technology helped modernize farming and ranching, establish new industries, and improve transportation across the country. Outside Asunción, rural communities, joined in some instances by immigrants from overseas, produced good yields of staple foods as well as export crops. Foreign companies invested in the republic, although they were often criticized for taking over the best farmland and the country's natural resources.

This period of peace came to an end when a border dispute with Bolivia developed into full-scale war. Military service was made compulsory, foreign military personnel were brought in to train troops, and a military school was built.

A 1934 photograph of a Paraguay regiment during the Chaco War

Bolivia, the one other landlocked country in South America, lost its only access to the Pacific Ocean in a war with Chile in 1884. It saw the possibility of an alternative by way of the Río de la Plata system to the Atlantic Ocean, but this entailed having control of the Chaco region. Also there were rumors of oil in the Chaco. For its part, Paraguay was happy at the prospect of redeeming its reputation after the War of the Triple Alliance.

Hostilities broke out when a Bolivian force stormed a Paraguayan fort in June 1932. The Bolivians expected an easy victory. They had superior numbers, considerable wealth generated from tin mines, and a German-trained army, but they had not considered the Paraguayan leadership of President Eusebio Ayala and General José Felix Estigarribia. The war dragged on for three years, and once again the casualties from the fighting and from disease ran into tens of thousands. When eventually a peace treaty was signed in 1938, over three-quarters of the Chaco was awarded to Paraguay, but the country was once again in ruins.

Colonel Rafael Franco (far left)
seized the presidency in 1936
but he was deposed and
José Felix Estigarribia (left)
became president in 1939.

MORE DICTATORS

For another twenty years, Paraguay lived with a series of
dictators, political instability, and very little progress. The first to
be removed were the Liberals, who had done nothing to help the
peasants. A new president, Colonel Rafael Franco, seized power in
1936. His supporters, the *Febreristas,* took their name from the
month in which the coup took place. Franco introduced land
reform by breaking up some large estates and giving the peasants
their own small plots of land, and he allowed trade unions and
the right to strike. Even so, he too was deposed.

The war hero José Felix Estigarribia became president in 1939,
ready to expand on the Febreristas' program. He was concerned
about the social and political situation. He introduced a new
constitution that allowed for an elected legislature and an
advisory council of state with representatives from commerce, the
church, and the military. The constitution gave all Paraguayans
over eighteen years of age the right to vote. A fatal plane crash put

After Estigarribia was killed in a plane crash, Higinio Morínigo became president.

an early end to Estigarribia's attempts at reform. He was succeeded by Higinio Morínigo, another Chaco War hero, who was clever, ruthless, and less caring than his predecessor.

Morínigo's time in power coincided with World War II. He assumed dictatorial powers, and being something of an opportunist, gave support to the Allies once he saw they were going to win, although his sympathies lay with the Axis powers of Germany and Italy.

Paraguay benefited from the war with increased trade in beef, hides, cotton, and timber. The republic also received considerable aid from the United States and Brazil, in return for cooperation in keeping an eye on Argentina, known to be backing the Axis powers. It was vital for the United States to have a strategic base close to Argentina.

In 1947 the Febreristas and Liberals joined together in an unsuccessful revolt against Morínigo. The following year, Morínigo's own Colorado party deposed him, and elections in 1948 were won by Juan Natalicio González. He did not stay in

Federico Chávez (left) was removed from the presidency by a coup and General Alfredo Stroessner (right) became dictator with the title of president from 1954 until 1989.

power long, and Dr. Federico Chávez, leader of the Colorado party, became provisional president in 1949. Chávez won the presidential election in 1953, but in turn was removed by a coup that brought to power General Alfredo Stroessner.

GENERAL ALFREDO STROESSNER

Alfredo Stroessner was dictator of Paraguay from 1954 until he was deposed in 1989, by which time he was the longest-ruling dictator in modern Latin America and the second longest in the world.

His father was a German immigrant who settled in Encarnación and ran a beer factory. His mother was Paraguayan. The young Alfredo Stroessner joined the army and after a period in military college went to fight in the Chaco War, from which he emerged with commendations and medals and a reputation as a good leader. Promoted to major, he married Doña Eligia and they had three children. By the age of thirty-three Stroessner was commander of Paraguay's chief artillery unit and played a prominent part in crushing the unsuccessful revolt of 1947. About that time he associated himself with the Colorado party. In 1951 Stroessner was appointed commander-in-chief of the armed forces. Three years later Stroessner was president of the republic.

In the beginning there was an almost universal welcome for anyone able to ensure political stability and a period of peace in Paraguay. But it soon became apparent that Stroessner was no different from many of his predecessors and was prepared to use any means to enforce his own authoritarian rule. Public employees found, for example, that a percentage of their salary was deducted as a compulsory contribution to the Colorado party. In every office and shop the government had an informer, known as a *pyrague*, a Guaraní word meaning a "man with hair on the soles of his feet"—in other words, silent footsteps.

Opponents of Stroessner were imprisoned, tortured, or exiled. He restricted all political activity and used the military to put down any form of revolt. Paraguay lived under an almost continuous state of siege. Newspapers and radio stations were closed and only the church managed consistently to criticize the regime. In the 1960s the church gave its support to a nonviolent peasant movement whose aim was to get a fair distribution of land, with the result that the government invaded church property and the archbishop of Asunción refused to take part in the council of state. The peasant movement itself was persecuted later when the government accused it of being associated with a guerrilla movement among left-wing students. Fifty peasant leaders were killed and some five thousand arrested.

A degree of political opposition was gradually allowed during

President Stroessner in 1968

the 1960s, but not enough to realistically challenge the Colorado party and Stroessner's own position. Stroessner was thus "reelected" regularly every five years, twice changing the constitution to make it possible to succeed himself. His presence was everywhere. Towns, bridges, buildings, and the international airport were named after him. His portrait hung in offices and flashed in neon lights on city buildings. Stroessner used foreign aid and loans from the United States and international banks to build schools and hospitals, improve the country's roads and transport system, and turn Asunción into a modern capital. When he came to power, less than one square mile of Asunción had running water, and water and milk were sold from mule carts. Today much has changed and Asunción resembles any commercial city in the Western world.

Among the people to benefit most from these changes, however, were those associated with the president—the army and the Colorado party. A few families became wealthy; they lived in

Construction begins on the Itaipú Dam

mansions on vast estates and owned fleets of luxury cars. There was widespread corruption, subsequently made much worse by the trade in drugs and cocaine that invaded the Andean part of South America in the 1980s. Paraguay was the ideal place from which to organize contraband operations. There are many small, hidden airstrips in the Chaco, and provided the payoff was good, no questions were asked. Smuggling became the country's number-one business.

Paraguay also became the exiled home of many of the world's right-wing extremists, drug traffickers, deposed leaders, and dozens of common criminals. The most infamous was the Nazi war criminal Josef Mengele, responsible for the death of thousands of Jews. More recently Anastasio Somoza, the hated dictator of Nicaragua, was traced to a wealthy suburb of Asunción, where he was gunned down.

In the late 1970s, when Paraguay and Brazil were building the Itaipú Dam, the country experienced an unprecedented economic boom, with one of the highest growth rates in the world. But once

After Stroessner was ousted in 1989, happy Paraguayans celebrated. The poster reads: "Hello dear Democracy— Liberty at last—They have arrived."

the first stage of the dam was completed in 1982, the boom began to fade, and other projects Stroessner had in mind did not materialize. People close to Stroessner say that at this time he seemed to lose his grip. Division began to emerge in the Colorado party, with traditionalists on one side and militants on the other. The traditionalists eventually triumphed and the coup, when it occurred in February 1989, apparently took Stroessner by surprise. He was allowed to go into exile in Brazil.

INTO THE 1990s

The coup was led by General Andrés Rodríguez, one of the nation's richest men. Rodríguez was commander of the first army and one of President Stroessner's closest confidants. His daughter married Stroessner's son. When he assumed power, Rodríguez's association with Stroessner made it difficult for Paraguayans to

General Andrés Rodríguez signs in as provisional president of Paraguay.

take his pledges of restoring democracy seriously. But there was optimism when the new government took immediate steps to normalize relations with the church, legalized the opposition parties (with the exception of the Communist party), invited many exiles to return, allowed newspapers and radio stations to reopen, and called for democratic elections. The opposition parties were dismayed that the government allowed only ninety days to prepare for the elections, because unlike the Colorado party, they were not organized for such an event after thirty-five years of suppression. The result of the election, amid accusations of fraud, was an inevitable victory for General Rodríguez and the Colorado party.

The government faces economic and social problems. There is a conflict over land ownership, with 80 percent in the hands of 1 percent of landowners, many of them foreigners who were encouraged to invest at the time of the Itaipú construction.

A rally of the Colorado party

Stroessner's regime gave away some land to the peasants, and the problem now is to find sufficient land for others who have threatened violence if nothing is done.

GOVERNMENT

The government of Paraguay is based on the constitution that took effect after the presidential election of 1968. The president of the republic must be a Roman Catholic over forty years old, and he is elected for a five-year term. He is also commander-in-chief of the armed forces and has extensive powers, which include the appointment of ministers, the administration of foreign affairs, and the authority to call a state of siege and dissolve Congress.

The president also appoints a Council of State that acts in an advisory capacity. Its members are ministers of government, the rector of the national university, and representatives of agriculture, manufacturing, commerce, labor, banking, and the armed forces.

The Legislative Palace in Asunción
with a statue of Juan de Salazar, the founder of Asunción

Legislative power is vested in a Congress made up of the Senate with thirty-six members and the Chamber of Deputies with sixty members. Congress is elected for five years, and the party with a majority of votes in the presidential election—which since 1948 has been the Colorado party—gets two-thirds of the seats in the Senate and the Chamber of Deputies.

The Supreme Court is made up of five members who are appointed for five years by the president. The court has the power to declare legislation unconstitutional.

The country is divided into nineteen administrative departments, each headed by a government delegate who is appointed by the president.

In 1977 an amendment to the constitution allowed for the president to be eligible for election for more than two consecutive terms of office.

Above: Macá Indians (above) and cowboys (right)
in their traditional dress at a fiesta
Below: Shopping at an outdoor market and
a mother with her child (bottom right)

Chapter 5

THE PEOPLE OF
PARAGUAY

Two important factors have influenced the way in which the population of Paraguay has developed since the Spanish arrived. The first has been the periodic isolation of the country and the second the large number of men killed in the War of the Triple Alliance and the Chaco War. After each war there was a generation of predominantly women and children. Present figures show there is once again about the same number of each sex. The population at 4.3 million is still small in relation to the size of the country, but the growth rate in 1990 of 2.7 percent is one of the highest in South America.

There is a small population of blacks on the border with Brazil and a relatively small number of foreigners who arrived in the twentieth century, including some Mennonites, members of a religious community who have settled in the Chaco.

Many factors over the centuries contributed to the demise of the native Indian peoples, of whom no more than forty thousand survive today. They are scattered throughout the country to make a living as best they can.

MESTIZOS

There is very little difference culturally or racially in the mestizos of Paraguay, who make up by far the greatest part of the

*The majority of Paraguayans are poor. Some live
in shacks like these beside the Río Paraguay.*

population. In many ways the Paraguayans present a
homogeneous society in attitude, dress, and language, particularly
because the most distinctive Indian feature of the mestizos of
Paraguay is that the majority are bilingual. Almost everyone
speaks both Spanish and Guaraní, and for many people, Guaraní
is their first language, particularly in the rural communities.
Guaraní is the familiar language, spoken among friends and
relatives, widely used in literature and the theater, and is the
language of the football field. As one poet wrote, "The
Paraguayans love, hate, and fight in Guaraní."

But the language, while being a common bond, has not totally
removed the distinctions drawn according to wealth, social, and
political standing or between rural and urban dwellers. The rich
are represented by the oligarchy, or landowning classes, and those
few families who for political or commercial reasons have become
extremely wealthy in recent years. The majority of people are
poor, and there is little they can do to bridge the huge gap that

exists between the levels of society. The wealthy and powerful have little interest in effecting any kind of change that might prove detrimental to their small, close society.

Most people recognize that there are greater opportunities and better facilities in Asunción and the towns. There has been an increasing movement from rural areas to urban centers. In 1990 only Bolivia had a higher urban growth rate than the 4 percent recorded in Paraguay. Newcomers to the urban centers generally have to accept the lowest form of social standing and work, but in dress and outlook they are much the same as working classes anywhere else on the continent. They may work as bus or taxi drivers, hotel porters, maids or office cleaners, or, if unable to find regular employment, many become street traders with stalls of duty-free or contraband goods. The better-off mestizo looks for work within the professions, such as teaching or medicine, but chances rest largely on the amount of education, now being improved throughout the country.

IMMIGRANTS

The few attempts by immigrants to settle in the nineteenth century came to nothing. There were groups from France, England, Australia, Italy, and Germany.

The group from England was lured by a scheme intended to attract farmers from Lincolnshire, a rural county in England. But the unscrupulous contractors who were being paid to recruit the immigrants did not bother to go to Lincolnshire, and instead collected eight hundred people from the East End of London and shipped them off to Asunción. As city people, they did not stand a chance in the wilds of Paraguay and most died from illness.

The Australian attempt failed for different reasons. Whereas the setting up of the community was quite successful, with houses constructed and fields under cultivation, the people became discontent with the socialist-style rules and regulations that dominated the running of this "New Australia." Life for the women in particular was lonely and hard, and in the end people just drifted away to start a new life elsewhere.

There are just a few survivors today from what was perhaps the most bizarre attempt at colonization. In 1887, Elizabeth Nietzsche, who was the sister of the great German philosopher and a fervent anti-Semite, decided to create a colony of people of pure Aryan blood, a "master race" in the middle of Paraguay. The whole idea was little more than an ego trip for Elizabeth, who one writer has described as a "remarkably nasty woman." About 150 people paid to follow her. A large house was built for Elizabeth and a few small homes for some of the colonists. Some attempt to grow crops was made with a little trading with villages upriver, but little else was achieved. Word got back to Germany, where she was accused of being a sham and a swindler. Furious, Elizabeth left the colony and the people to their own devices. By 1906, about half the original number were still alive and a handful of their fair-haired descendants still survive today.

European arrivals in the twentieth century were more successful and found agricultural colonies that have thrived in the eastern part of the country. These colonists included Germans, Russians, and East Europeans. More recent immigrants have not come from Europe, but from Korea, Japan, and China. There was also an influx of colonists from Brazil at the time of the construction of the Itaipú Dam.

Houses in the Mennonite community near Filadelfia

THE MENNONITES

Easily the best-known foreign community is that of the German-speaking Mennonites, a religious sect that originated in Northern Europe in the sixteenth century. In the 1920s, when Mennonites from Canada and Russia were looking for a new home, they were offered land, tax incentives, and immigration advantages to encourage them to settle in the Chaco, which the Paraguayan government wanted to develop. The sect was free to run their community according to their own rules, which include no military service and having their own schools. They founded three colonies, Menno in 1926 with 1,743 people, Fernheim in 1930 with 2,000 people, and the most recent, Neuland, founded in 1947 with 2,400 people. Their population today has risen to more than 12,000.

At first the going was tough. In the scrub wilderness of the Chaco, there were hostile Indians and wild animals. Diseases like

Mennonites celebrating a religious festival

typhoid claimed many victims. The colonists persevered, building houses and churches and clearing the land for cultivation and crops. The Chaco War in the 1930s gave the Mennonites their first real contact with Paraguayans. They used military equipment that had been abandoned to make farm implements. In time, helped with funds from Mennonites in the United States, schools and hospitals were built, and in 1947 the first airstrip was completed. There was further communication with the outside world when the telephone system was installed, and recently the all-weather Trans-Chaco Highway was completed connecting the main center, Filadelfia, and other towns with Asunción.

Donations also helped provide the Mennonites with a firm economic base. Initially their main produce was cotton, peanut oil, and other extracts. Today they have a thriving dairy cattle industry, and within the Fernheim colony alone there are 114,000 head of cattle. Dairy products include milk, yogurt, and butter that are sold in Asunción, together with cheese, which since 1990 has been exported to Brazil. There is a UHT plant in Loma Plata near Filadelfia where long-life milk is produced by a process of ultrahigh temperature sterilization.

Within the communities all social and cultural needs are taken care of, from old people's homes to sports clubs. A radio station used to spread the religious word broadcasts in seven languages.

One result of Mennonite success has been to attract Indians from the Chaco looking for work. Initially they were employed only as agricultural laborers, and since the early 1960s the Mennonites have set up agricultural colonies, with medical and educational facilities for the Indians. In many ways the Indians are better off, but they feel trapped into an existence that will only give them second-class status. Recent economic changes in the Chaco, however, have driven thousands more Indians to seek refuge and work in Filadelfia, a problem that is becoming increasingly more difficult for the small community to handle.

THE INDIANS

Native Indians now represent only a small fraction of Paraguay's population. Perhaps forty thousand have survived, representing seventeen tribes and belonging to five different language groups. Despite the decline due to the Spanish conquest, disease, and wars, the greatest struggle for Indian survival has occurred in the years since the War of the Triple Alliance.

Faced with huge debts after the war, the government sold off vast tracts of land, often to foreign companies. Since then, more land assumed to be owned by the state has been sold to speculators or has been redistributed as part of a land reform program. Indians, who perhaps for generations had their homes on these lands but with no legal rights of ownership, have been driven off or forced out.

In east Paraguay there are four surviving tribes of Indians. The worst problems for them occurred in the 1960s and 1970s when the government was anxious to sell to the thousands of Brazilians who were flooding across the border into Paraguay to buy land. The Aché-Guayakí tribe suffered very badly, as they were primarily nomadic hunter gatherers and very reliant on the forest. They were hunted down, enslaved, or killed. Many died from epidemics. By the end of the 1970s, almost all of the Aché had abandoned their forest life. Most of the remaining members of the tribe now live in two settlements and a reserve with missionaries. Others are scattered through east Paraguay.

The other three tribes, who are more sedentary and agriculture based, live in widely scattered communities where they grow crops and hunt. When possible, they get part-time labor on farms and settlements.

In the Chaco, large areas of land were sold off soon after the War of the Triple Alliance, even though the Indians fought fiercely to resist the intrusion. It was an ironic twist of fate that one Anglican missionary, W. Barbrooke Grubb, was so successful in overcoming Indian hostility in the region that he made it easier for exploitation to continue. The remarkable Mr. Grubb was given the title "Pacifier of the Indians" by the Paraguayan government, who made him their legal representative in the Chaco for eighteen years.

Since then, the Chaco War, the Mennonites, and the Trans-Chaco Highway have all played a part in opening up the region. Today most Indians have been forced to abandon their traditional

*Only a small portion
of Paraguayans
are native Indians.
Some surviving
tribes are the
Aché-Guayakí (top left),
the Macá (above),
and the Chaco (left).*

way of life and have become part of the cash economy, working as
commercial hunters and as farm laborers. Some of the more
fortunate have lands held in their name by missionaries and other
organizations, but the majority own nothing.

Exceptionally, one tribe, the Macá, were given an island site
close to Asunción in the 1940s by a local patron. The eight
hundred or so members of the tribe now live by selling
handicrafts and receiving tourists into their villages.

Above: The heart of Asunción is the Plaza de los Héroes.
Below: The Presidential Palace

Asunción

Chapter 6

LIVING AND WORKING IN PARAGUAY

ASUNCIÓN

None of the public buildings in Asunción is very old; most date
from the nineteenth century. Some of the grandest were
commissioned by Carlos Antonio López and his son and were
influenced in design by European engineers and architects. The
splendid Government Palace, also known as the López Palace, is
built in the style of the Louvre in Paris and is surrounded by well-
cut lawns and ornamental shrubs. The president has his office in
the palace and holds state receptions there. Nearby in another
park stands the imposing Legislative Palace, built between 1842
and 1851, with a fine view of the river and the cathedral.

The central area of the city is built on a traditional Spanish grid
system of avenues and cross-streets that in July and August are
vividly colored with pink lapacho trees. At the heart of this part of
the city is the Plaza de los Héroes with the tiny though impressive

The Pantheon (left) contains tombs of Carlos Antonio and Francisco Solano López, José Felix Estigarribia, and two unknown soldiers killed in battle. Soldiers in dress uniform (above) guard the entrance.

National Pantheon de los Héroes. The domed Pantheon, based on Les Invalides in Paris, contains the tombs of Carlos Antonio and Francisco Solano López and other heroes of Paraguay, and is guarded by a perpetual flame of remembrance and two immaculately uniformed soldiers.

A few blocks to the east are the Plaza Uruguay and the Carlos Antonio López railway station built in 1861. Here at 12:15 P.M. each day a vintage British-built steam locomotive leaves the station with a short train bound for the villages around Lake Ypacaraí, twenty-five miles (forty kilometers) to the east. Preparations for the trip begin with stacking the tender high with wood to fire the locomotive. Then steam, smoke, and sparks are blown everywhere as with a long blast on the whistle the train pulls away from the platform. Just beyond the ornate station portico the railway line crosses a busy road and all traffic waits for the train to pass. The passengers wave as the carriages clatter

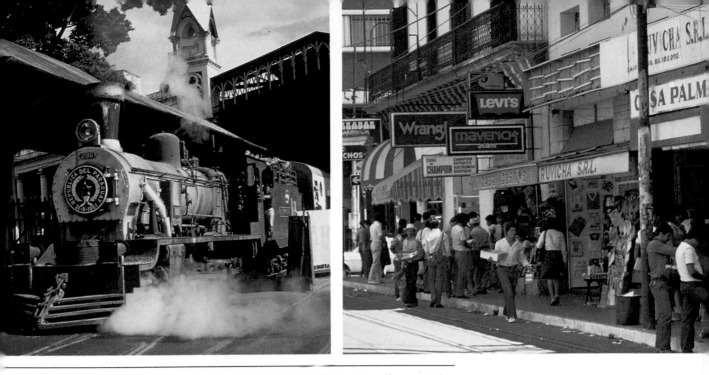

*A wood-burning locomotive leaves the main railway station
in Asunción (left); Palma Street (right) is always
crowded with shoppers.*

along between the houses and pedestrians who watch quite
casually as the train has been running on time for many years.

Other historic buildings in the city include the one-story,
whitewashed *Casa de la Independencia,* or "House of
Independence," which dates from 1772, and is now a museum
containing many colonial relics.

Ancient streetcars and brightly colored buses rumble along two
of Asunción's main streets at the center of the commercial life of
the city. Always crowded with people, Palma Street is where most
of the street vendors, money exchange houses, and numerous
banks are located. Many of them are international names, and in
recent years high-rise blocks have begun to dominate the skyline,
replacing the old one and two-story buildings that used to line the
street.

In the blocks between Palma and Estrella streets, close to the
Plaza de los Héroes, are some of the major general stores for

Above: Street vendors sell many imported goods.
Inset: Electric streetcars are still in use in the capital.

imported goods. These shops offer items from all over the world at prices that are, perhaps, expensive for many Paraguayans but highly competitive with those of neighboring countries. Floors are devoted to fashions, perfumes, cloth, toys, garden and workshop tools, and many other goods. The stores are crowded with visitors and trade is always brisk.

On weekdays these streets are busy early as people arrive at work. In the plazas the shoe shiners are occupied and the coffee houses are filled. Then at noon central Asunción closes and for three and a half hours the streets are virtually empty. Even the streetcars stop and everyone takes time for lunch and a siesta until

A residential section next to the downtown area.

between three or four o'clock in the afternoon, when the city comes alive again. Shopping continues until late at night. On Saturdays Palma Street is closed to traffic and vendors cram the pavements with stalls containing every kind of handicraft and trinket. Women work their way along the streets with piles of fruit in baskets balanced on their heads or selling snacks. From the center the city has spread in every direction, especially along the major routes leading out of town. Avenida Mariscal López, the road to the airport, is lined with many stylish residences, while other roads pass through a neighborhood of poorer though substantial housing.

Friendship Bridge and a view of Ciudad del Este from Brazil

AT WORK IN THE COUNTRY

In the cities outside Asunción, many people also are involved in trading, particularly in the ports on the Río Paraná. Ciudad del Este, founded in the 1950s, already has a population of 100,000 and gives an impression of being half finished. Shops, hotels, and apartments are still being built to accommodate the hundreds of Brazilian tourists who daily cross Friendship Bridge over the Río Paraná linking Brazil and Paraguay. The city relies on these tourists who buy all kinds of imported goods, including cameras, whiskey and other spirits, and watches and electronic gadgets of all kinds from shops and street traders. Prices are far lower than in Brazil and each tourist is permitted to return with a generous quota of purchases. The tourist trade is similar in Encarnación, except the visitors are Argentines and the variety of goods is not as great. In both towns people are relatively prosperous, finding work in transportation, packing, and export.

Encarnación

Around Encarnación in the south farming is well developed and conducted on a large scale, with both cattle and crops. People are employed on the farms as cowboys and farmhands, producing a variety of agricultural products including soybeans, tobacco, yerba maté, tung oil, cotton, and hides.

Elsewhere in the countryside, particularly closer to Asunción, peasant farmers have a hard life. The majority do not own any land. Some rent from landowners, but most are squatters who need to find other part-time work or a trade to make ends meet. Even the few who have managed to acquire some acres have an uphill struggle, as the plots are generally too small to be economic. Rural families are usually large, with several generations sharing one dwelling, and everyone is expected to help with the farm work. Typically a family may farm one or two acres of land on which they have their houses, a small barn for storage, and a pen for pigs. Chickens are allowed to run freely except at night.

A farmer cultivates his soybeans.

As the first aim of the farmer is to provide food for his family, the plot is planted with manioc, maize, melons, tomatoes, and lettuce. Rice, wheat, and some potatoes are also grown. Many small farms have trees that produce oranges, limes, holly, and yerba maté, and these may provide a surplus for local sale.

While they may produce enough to feed themselves, the small farmers can in no way compete with the larger, more mechanized farms. With virtually no mechanical equipment to make their work easier, small farmers have to rely on oxen to plow the fields, to work presses to extract the juice from the sugarcane, and to transport produce to and from town. One way in which the small farmer can be helped, and the government has supported the idea, is by the formation of cooperatives, through which mechanical equipment can be bought and shared by a group of farmers.

A house in San Juan Bautista

HOUSING

The construction of simple housing does not have to contend
with extremes of temperature, but rainfall has to be considered. In
rural areas houses may be built of adobe, brick, concrete blocks, or
timber, depending on the income of the family. Roofing may be of
tiles, palm thatch, or corrugated iron. In all but the poorest homes
a rural house has several rooms and perhaps even a shower room,
though in country places these are often set apart from the house.
In some places cooking is still done on an open fire, and bread is
baked in a dome-shaped mud oven outside the home.

Some of the poorest homes are those of squatters who live in
hastily erected shacks with no water or light and of Indians such
as the Ayoreo of the Chaco who have adopted a semiurban life
and own little more than plastic-covered shelters slung between
trees.

Houses in towns and villages are quite substantial. Some houses
are next to one another on a street, Spanish style, or are set apart

Houses owned by the wealthy overlooking the Río Paraguay at Asunción

in small plots. Piped water and electricity are no longer rare, though not all homes are connected to a main sewer.

In Asunción homes can range from the poorest wood-and-metal shacks crammed together to luxury air-conditioned mansions surrounded by fine landscaped gardens. But by far the most obvious housing is the broad and frequently attractive range of apartments and single or two-story houses in the suburbs. The older streets are lined with well-constructed houses. There are gray buildings, often tinged green by tropical mold, with iron railings and ornate moldings that date to the beginning of the twentieth century.

Many of the poorer homes line the river edge. In years when the Río Paraguay is exceptionally high, the inhabitants have to leave their houses by boat with whatever they can salvage and build temporary housing higher up the steep bank.

Students relaxing in the Plaza de los Héroes

EDUCATION

The standard of education in Paraguay depends entirely on the region. Officially children have to attend school for six years, starting with the primary level when they are seven years old. Secondary school lasts for another six years, but very few children remain in school until they are eighteen. In 1986, 87 percent of the children were estimated to have attended primary school, with 25 percent at secondary level in the same year.

It is much easier for the children living in Asunción and the big towns to attend school, not only because there is plenty of transport but also because there are many more schools. Sometimes schools find they have to run double shifts so that all the children can attend.

High school girls at a spring festival

By contrast schools in the countryside are fewer and not as well equipped. Parents in rural areas do not always encourage their children to attend because they need the children to help on the farms, and children are often discouraged because they have to walk many miles to reach the nearest school.

The majority of schools are run by the state or by the church, but some are private. Subjects studied are taught in both Spanish and Guaraní. Successful students can go on to higher education, either to vocational schools for technical or agricultural training or to one of the two universities. Students of wealthy families often travel overseas to attend universities.

Although most people are bilingual in Spanish and Guaraní, well over 10 percent of adults still cannot read or write. The government is encouraging evening classes for older students in an effort to wipe out illiteracy.

HEALTH

Although medical clinics and hospitals in the rural areas, like schools, increased in number during the Stroessner years, there are still not enough to adequately service the population. Also like the schools, they are not well equipped, and it is difficult to attract qualified staff to work in the country areas where some health problems are common. Because Paraguay is in a subtropical zone, insect-borne disease is always a danger, and in recent years dengue fever has been reported. It is caused by a virus carried from person to person by a mosquito. Hookworm is the most common parasitical infestation and most often occurs when people walk barefoot in places where the hookworm larvae from untreated sewage are in the soil. Poor water supplies are another health hazard, and less than half of the population has access to safe water.

It is not surprising, under these conditions, that many peasant families still have great belief in their own herbal cures. With a rich variety of plants and a strong Indian heritage, Paraguayans use many medicinal herbs, including *batatilla*, a tuber from the potato family.

FOOD

Taking yerba maté is more than having a drink of refreshing tea. In Paraguay it is part of the way of life and has been so since long before the Spanish arrived. The Guaraní introduced it to the Spaniards, and Guaraní legends surround its origin. The story is told of Caá Yara, a beautiful young girl whose parents made her live in seclusion in the forest to protect her from the evils of the

A farmer checks his yerba tree (left),
and enjoys a yerba maté (above).

world. She was found disguised as a traveler by a Guaraní god
who, on learning of the parents' concern, made Caá Yara
immortal. Her spirit resides in the yerba tree—known in Guaraní
as *caá*.

The yerba leaves are picked by hand and dried on wooden racks
above a simple outdoor oven. The dried leaves are milled into a
fine powder that is mixed with water. The tea is traditionally
drunk from a *maté*, a vessel made from a vegetable gourd or cow
horn, and sipped through a *bombilla*, a sort of metal or wooden
drinking tube that works like a straw with a filter. Maté can be
drunk hot, or on warm days Paraguayans enjoy *terere*, which is
cold maté mixed with herbs. On social occasions, the maté is
passed around and everyone has a sip from the same bombilla. It
is an insult to refuse! In recent years Paraguayans, like their
neighbors in Uruguay and Argentina, have taken to carrying
vacuum flasks of water so they can top up their maté at any time.

A variety of fresh breads for sale

Paraguayans, particularly the country people, eat many different types of soups. The main ingredients are meat, vegetables, and cheese. The national dish is *sopa paraguaya*, which is not a soup but a kind of dumpling of ground maize and cheese. Maize is also used for *chipa soo*, maize bread filled with meat, while *chipas* are a yucca bread flavored with egg and cheese. A drink called *mosto* is sold from roadside stalls in the countryside. It is chilled sugarcane juice, freshly pressed and served undiluted.

Also popular in the countryside are *asados*, large-scale barbecues with huge cuts of beef skewered on poles and roasted over a charcoal fire in a pit. Meat is widely available. In the towns and cities *parrilladas*, or grills, are used to cook different types of meat over an open fire in homes and restaurants. Most recently, fast-food shops serving chicken and hamburgers have arrived in Asunción.

Although fish is plentiful, people catch only what they need to

A street vendor sells grilled kabobs of various meats.

eat or sell in the market. Particularly delicious and served in a variety of ways is surubi, a catfish that weighs 40 to 50 pounds (18 to 23 kilograms). In country areas surubi is salted and dried to preserve it for future meals. Other fish commonly eaten are the bagre, the corvina, and the paku, though perhaps the most popular is the dorado.

RELIGION

Since the Spanish conquest the majority of Paraguayan people have officially belonged to the Roman Catholic church. There are regular church services, and important religious occasions such as Christmas and Easter are celebrated in accordance with the Christian calendar.

There is great respect, also, for local patron saints, and annual festivities are held in their honor. On a feast day, a statue of the saint, colorfully decorated with streamers and flowers, is carried in a procession around the village or town. Every year in early December thousands of pilgrims flock to the shrine of the Basilica of Our Lady of the Miracles in Caacupé to celebrate with candlelit processions, fireworks, and the national "bottle dance."

The seventeenth-century Franciscan church at Yaguarón

Since the days of the Jesuits, missionaries and others have been directly involved with education and welfare among the people. Among a variety of small and large colonial churches, the Franciscan church at Yaguarón is outstanding in its architecture and beautiful wood carvings.

The relationship between the church and the state, however, has often been difficult, from the days when Dr. Francia, soon after independence, sought to remove the church's power and possessions, to the Stroessner regime, when the church was the only organization able to openly criticize the government. It took considerable courage on the part of the archbishop of Asunción and other church leaders to express their opposition to the dictatorship. Their actions served to make the world aware of the lack of freedom in Paraguay. When Pope John Paul II visited the country in 1988, some of the people at one of his meetings were televised wearing masks over their mouths to symbolize their inability to speak freely.

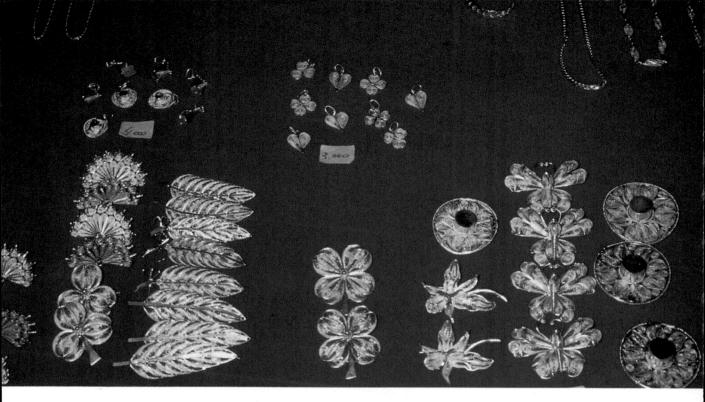

Silver filigree jewelry (top) and section of a wall hanging by
the artist Bouman, showing the Pantheon de los Héroes,
representing Paraguay's colonial past (below)

Chapter 7

ART AND CULTURE

THE CULTURAL TRADITION

Guaraní legend and tradition are present in Paraguayan culture and embrace many aspects of the arts. The Indians' artistic talents were first realized in the Jesuit missions, where they were taught to paint and carve and where they learned to play new musical instruments introduced from Europe. For many years after the expulsion of the Jesuits, through independence and the years of isolation that followed, there was little development of any cultural tradition. It was not until the end of the nineteenth century that a national literature and art emerged, with work that was often politically motivated.

Most Paraguayan artists and writers have taken their topics from events of local or national history or from the social conditions of their country. It is no coincidence that leading literary figures such as Cecilio Báez, Eusebio Ayala, and Juan Natalicio González were all presidents of the country.

Among the artists, Pablo Alborno helped establish the National Academy of Fine Arts in 1910, studied in Europe, and introduced impressionism into Paraguay. He specialized in murals, but his best-known work is *Nanduti Lacemakers*. Julián de la Herrería is known for his sympathetic paintings of Indians, and the impressionist Jaime Bestard in his paintings has depicted local fiestas, cockfights, and landscapes.

GUARANÍ WOODCARVERS

Not surprising, under the influence of the Jesuits, much of the work of the Guaraní artisans was dedicated to the greater glory of God. Many examples of Indian skills and Jesuit influence can still be seen today in magnificent brick-and-stone churches with paintings and finely worked carvings, statues, and pulpits in native woods.

In decoration and design the Indians often copied the flowers and fruits of the natural world, such as passion flowers, pineapples, palms, and ferns. Angels, their faces sculptured with distinctly Indian features, hung from the ceilings and pillars of churches, and altars were lavishly ornamented with skillfully fashioned silver candlesticks and plates.

The Guaraní also produced beautifully woven carpets and illuminated manuscripts. Throughout there was the strict discipline of Catholic teaching combined with the flair and originality of Indian craft.

Today some of the artistic talents of the local people near Encarnación are being employed in the careful reconstruction work at the ruined Jesuit mission at Trinidad. Stone masons and other experts have been cleaning and repairing the imposing structures built more than 250 years ago. Carvings, niches, and grand arches in stone are being painstakingly restored to preserve an extraordinary legacy of religious dedication.

A magnificent example of the work achieved by Indians under

The Jesuits encouraged the Guaraní to use their talents and skills. The pulpit (above) and the angel (below) are examples of the beautiful carving done by the Guaraní.

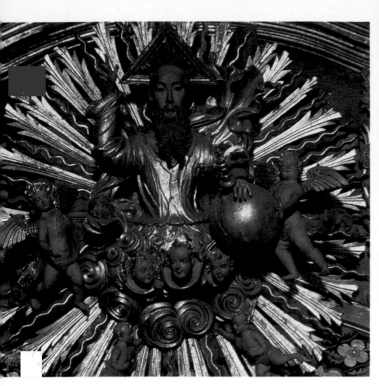

A Guaraní carving in the interior of the Franciscan church in Yaguarón (left). A lace maker trims away surplus cloth on a section of nanduti lace (above).

Franciscan missionary instruction is the church at Yaguarón, built between 1670 and 1720. It is considered to be one of the finest Indian baroque churches in Spanish America. Quite plain on the outside, the interior is filled with delicately painted and gilded wooden carvings on columns, ceilings, pillars, pews, and pulpits, and a magnificently elaborate altar.

LACE MAKERS OF ITAUGUÁ

The most famous and beautiful handicraft of Paraguay is nanduti lace. Lace making was introduced by the Spaniards, but the lace has a legendary Guaraní origin, based on the word *nanduti* which means "spiderweb." The legend tells of a Paraguayan girl who went in search of her lover when he did not appear on their wedding day. At nightfall she found his dead body in the forest, and on waking in the morning saw it covered

Finishing a nanduti lace tablecloth in Itauguá (above); the spiderweb pattern can be seen in the work in progress (above right).

by a mantle of shimmering spiderwebs. She hastened home, returned with a needle and thread, and copied the spiderweb patterns into a shroud, thus making the first piece of nanduti lace.

Today women weave the lace from a piece of cloth stretched onto a wooden frame, and they make up the design from any of a hundred or so different patterns. Some of the patterns relate to flowers, such as the jasmine; others to birds and animals, such as rhea plumage or owls' bills; or they may have an agricultural or religious significance, as in anthills in the cornfields and drapery for the cross. The weaver decides what patterns to use and women then finish the cloth by using manioc starch to stiffen the threads before trimming away any surplus cloth. The town of Itauguá is the center of the lace-making industry. The main road is lined with craft shops displaying nanduti in a wide variety of colors. Some of the largest pieces are tablecloths, while smaller examples of the fine work include place mats, collars and cuffs, or even *mantillas*, lace scarves or veils. For very special occasions, such as a confirmation or wedding, the lace is used to create beautiful dresses.

Cotton spinning and weaving are two traditional handicrafts, and *aho-poi* is a type of homespun cotton that the women hand embroider. It is sold in suitable lengths to make shirts or other garments or ready-made in the traditional style of off-the-shoulder blouses.

MUSIC AND DANCE

When the Spaniards arrived, the Jesuits encouraged the Guaraní to enjoy their love of music by teaching them to make and play European instruments such as the guitar, viola, and harp. They also introduced religious songs that the Indians would chant as they made their way daily to the fields. With the mixing of the two cultures, it is the Spanish music and dances that are most popular today.

The guitar and harp are Paraguay's national instruments, and the craft of making them has passed from father to son for generations. For the last thirty years, the guitar playing and folk songs of the Trio Los Paraguayos has been famous throughout the world. It is the harp, however, with its mellower tones, that particularly distinguishes Paraguayan music. Two leading harpists are Felix Perez Cardoso and Gigno Garcia.

Dances include the polka, waltz, and galop, and there are many folk dances including the Santa Fé, which resembles an American square dance, and the Pericón, a traditional dance from Spain in which a man recites a poem and his partner has to make a suitable reply in rhyme. The most famous folk dance is the "bottle dance"

A band featuring the famous Paraguayan harp

in which a pyramid of bottles is balanced on the dancer's head, with the top bottle sometimes carrying a spray of flowers. Not a petal is dropped by the most expert dancers despite their quite vigorous movements.

Music and dance have always been important to the native tribes as part of their ritual and for relaxation. The Indians have traditionally made most of their instruments in natural materials from the forests and rivers around them. Among Chaco tribes, strings of rattles, which are tied around the ankles, are made from deer hooves, fruit rind, turtle shell, and other materials; gourds are filled with seeds or pebbles; and the Indians have a variety of flutes made from wood and cane. Some make panpipes and there are trumpetlike instruments, one of which is used to attract fish.

Young men playing soccer (left) and a comic bullfight (right)

SPORT

The most popular sport in Paraguay is soccer, which is played at the international, national, and local level. Every town or village has a team, and any spare hours are spent kicking a ball around on whatever ground is available. Paraguay competes with other South American countries in the qualifying round of the World Cup and other competitions. Basketball and rugby football are enjoyed too.

There are facilities for other sports, including tennis, and an eighteen-hole golf course in Asunción, although many of these are restricted to those people who can afford them. The rivers and lakes provide ample opportunity for water sports. There are also swimming and rowing clubs, as well as a motorboat club. Paraguayans are traditionally skilled horsemen, and rodeos are greatly enjoyed as a family outing. Sometimes, in rural areas, there are comic bullfights, when villagers dress in masks and costume and climb into the ring to challenge the bull, though without actually harming it. Such events are often accompanied by a delicious asado, after which there is music and dancing late into the night.

Chapter 8

THE ECONOMY

Paraguay shares many of the problems of developing countries. It suffers from inflation and from high unemployment and underemployment, has few products suitable for export, and is burdened with debts owed to international banks and organizations. There are problems that are beyond the country's control. Floods or drought frequently affect crop production, while the value of the country's limited exports can rise or fall according to prices set on the world market. Prior to 1970 the country was one of the poorest and least developed on the continent. In the 1980s and 1990s Paraguay has done better than most of its neighbors. There was considerable growth in the gross domestic product, real wages rose, exports outstripped imports, and in 1990 the external debt was decreased by 19 percent.

The republic's improved fortunes were due to the construction of the Itaipú hydroelectric dam, which in turn led to a dramatic increase of activity in the construction industry. At the same time there was a rapid expansion of agricultural production for export.

Paraguay's economic future continues to look bright with the completion of the Itaipú Dam. This should not only ensure ongoing high revenue on energy exported to Brazil but will provide Paraguay with all the energy it needs to develop its own manufacturing industries. For the time being, however, the mainstay of the Paraguay economy is agriculture. In that sector the country still faces some tough problems.

AGRICULTURE

Paraguay is a fertile country, with about one-fifth of the total land area suitable for intensive cultivation. Almost 40 percent of the working population is employed in agriculture, but the allocation of land is still a major problem.

For many years Paraguay's economy was dependent on the export of tannin, meat products, yerba maté, and tobacco. Today agriculture still accounts for 90 percent of exports. The two most important commodities are cotton and soybeans.

Other cash crops include cane sugar, wheat, tobacco, and various oils. Among these are tung oil, used in waterproofing cloth, varnishes, and soap making. Another important oil is taken from the leaves of bitter orange trees and used by the cosmetic industry in perfumes and soaps.

Although yerba maté is much less important than it used to be, it is still exported to neighboring South American countries because maté made from the wild trees of southern Paraguay is said to have a better flavor than that from cultivated plantations.

Cattle raising, which takes place mainly in the Chaco, has declined in importance. The market for canned, chilled, and frozen meat products declined and two major meat-canning

Sugarcane being transported in an ox-drawn cart

operations closed as the European Community cut back on its import quotas.

TIMBER AND MANUFACTURING INDUSTRIES

Before the 1970s about half the land of Paraguay was covered in forest. Since then extensive deforestation has caused a serious environmental problem. The forests have been cleared partly due to the need for agricultural land and partly because of the increased exploitation of timber for commercial and domestic purposes. The problem has become sufficiently severe for the government to pass legislation banning the export of logs to Brazil, the main market. Many of the sawmills on the border have closed. However, sawn timber in 1989 still represented 8 percent of total exports. One estimate suggests that at the current rate of deforestation, Paraguay's forests could disappear completely by 2028, but many people disagree with this pessimistic view.

Tiles to be used in construction are baked in an oven (kiln) at a factory.

The manufacturing industry traditionally has been dependent on agriculture. It is still relatively small, employing only 15 percent of the labor force, with almost three-quarters of the employees in concerns of less than twenty workers. There is little incentive to increase manufacturing for the domestic market because of the extensive smuggling of consumer goods from neighboring countries.

The main industries are meat and timber processing, textiles and cotton ginning (the removal of seeds from the cotton), and plants for extracting oil, vegetables, and quebracho, from which tannin is taken to tan animal hides. Most of these industries are based in Asunción.

The development of hydroelectric power led to the country's first steel mill, which provides light steel goods for the construction industry. Paraguay now has its own cement industry. The state runs these enterprises, together with a small shipbuilding industry and an operation for producing alcohol for fuel from sugarcane. However, the manufacturing sector remains small.

Visitors are dwarfed by the spillway of the Itaipú in 1991,
before it began operating.

MINING AND HYDROELECTRICITY

As the Spaniards discovered, Paraguay has few mineral
resources. The mining industry is limited to the extraction of
gypsum and limestone near the Río Paraguay, malachite and
azurite (two copper ores) near Caapucú, marble, kaolin, and salt.
Prospecting for oil and gas has taken place for many years but
with little result. Both state-owned and foreign companies have
concessions and there is active exploration in the Chaco and east
Paraguay.

Paraguay's rich resource lies in its rivers and their potential for
hydroelectricity. The Itaipú Dam was begun in 1973 and by 1982
when the first stage was completed had cost $18 billion. By May
1991 when the eighteenth and final turbine was in place, Itaipú
became the largest hydroelectric dam in the world. It has a main

The Itaipú hydroelectric dam in operation

concrete dam about half the height of the Empire State Building in New York, a powerhouse about 3,000 feet (more than 900 meters) long containing the largest turbine generators ever made, and an output of 12,500 megawatts. In the process of construction a reservoir was created that covered an area of 564 square miles (1,460 square kilometers) of farmland and forests, causing the transfer of some thirty thousand people and a great deal of wildlife. It also spelled the end for the Guaíra Falls on the Río Paraná.

The building of the dam also had a dramatic effect on the economy of the surrounding region. Between 1975 and 1978 an average of 15,000 Paraguayans were employed on the site. The workers and their families were provided with food, accommodations, and medical and educational facilities. Unemployment in the area was virtually unknown. People had money to spend and this fueled a big increase in the import of consumer goods. By 1990 the population of the region, including some 400,000 Brazilian colonists, represented about 20 percent of Paraguay's total population.

Brazil, supported by international banks, supplied most of the funds for the dam, and both countries contributed labor. The energy output is divided equally between the two, but it was obvious from the start that Paraguay would have much more than it needed, whereas Brazil needed all it could get for its 150 million population. It was agreed that Paraguay would sell back its surplus energy to Brazil at preferential rates. This has led to some discord between the two countries because Paraguay believes it is receiving too little payment and would like to sell some of the electricity to Argentina at market rates.

A joint project is now under way with Argentina to build a dam at Yacyretá downstream from Itaipú where the Río Paraná forms the border between the two countries. When completed, the surplus energy from Yacyretá together with that from Itaipú will make Paraguay one of the world's largest exporters of electricity with the prospect of considerable foreign earnings for many years to come.

TOURISM

Tourism is also an important foreign exchange earner, but revenue from this source is dependent on the economic situation in Paraguay's neighboring countries. It is not the conventional tourism of beautiful beaches and sun that attracts thousands of visitors. Tourism in this instance means the many thousands of short-stay people who cross into Paraguay to buy the low-priced consumer and electrical goods on offer in Encarnación, Ciudad del Este, and Asunción.

Chapter 9

PARAGUAY AND
THE WORLD

INTERNATIONAL TRADE

Paraguay's main trading partners are Brazil, Argentina, and the United States. Although Paraguay is now virtually self-sufficient in foodstuffs, it needs to import machinery, transportation and agricultural equipment, and all its petroleum requirements. Trading also takes place with Europe, although European Community restrictions have affected Paraguay's meat exports.

During the 1980s Paraguay's foreign debt to international banks and other organizations increased considerably until in 1987 it reached over 50 percent of the gross national product. Repayment on some of these loans seriously reduced the country's reserves. In 1990 Paraguay negotiated a rescheduling of its debts. A debt-swap made with Brazil for money owed to Paraguay against electricity led to a 19 percent reduction in the debt, which at the end of 1989 stood at $1.7 billion.

In an economic development plan, Paraguay has joined with its neighbors, Brazil, Argentina, and Uruguay, in the creation of a

The harbor at Asunción on the Río Paraguay

new economic bloc, Mercosur, which was inaugurated in March 1991. With a market of almost 200 million people the first aim is to reduce barriers between the four countries to allow for easier trade. It is hoped common policies can be developed in certain spheres, such as energy and transportation, that will lead to greater economic integration among the four nations.

TRANSPORTATION

In its landlocked position, a major problem for Paraguay has always been to ensure it has access to the sea, which essentially means remaining on good terms with Argentina and Brazil. Traditionally the route to the sea has been via the Paraguay, Paraná, and La Plata rivers to Buenos Aires. Asunción, on the Río Paraguay, is the country's largest port and the only one with modern facilities, though there are plans to develop another port 16 miles (26 kilometers) to the south of the capital. A vessel can make the approximately 1,000-mile (1,610-kilometer) journey

The Trans-Chaco Highway runs north from Asunción to the Bolivian border.

between Asunción and Buenos Aires in about a week. The Río Paraná is also navigable to the ports of Encarnación and Ciudad del Este.

Until recently 80 percent of Paraguay's imports and 40 percent of its exports were shipped through the Río de la Plata system, but an increasing amount of freight is now being transported overland to the Brazilian port of Paranaguá, where Paraguay has duty-free facilities. Another alternative route being considered is by river from the Itaipú lake into Brazil, to connect with a rail link to São Paulo.

International road links with neighboring countries have been improved. Entry into Brazil and Argentina has become easier with the construction of three bridges over the Río Paraná. Fast, comfortable long-distance buses have regular services connecting Asunción to the major towns in both countries.

The Trans-Chaco Highway is the only road from Asunción to the Bolivian border, a journey of 460 miles (740 kilometers). The

A plane from Líneas Aéreas Paraguayas at the main airport in Asunción

road is paved as far as Filadelfia, and the remainder of the route has a good firm surface. It seldom rains, but when it does, the road becomes so slippery that it is impassable. There are similar problems in other rural areas where few roads are paved and maintenance is costly and difficult. Floods are a constant problem and bridges frequently get washed away.

The railway network in Paraguay is very poor. On the one main line between Asunción and Encarnación, services are unreliable and sometimes out of action for months at a time. However, the line does connect with the Argentine system and improvements are being considered with a view to providing an alternative route for the export of agricultural products from the Villarrica region.

The national airline, Líneas Aéreas Paraguayas, has connections with all the major cities in South and Central America, and most parts of the world. Various international airlines fly into the country's main airport near Asunción. Previously known as the President Stroessner International Airport, it has now been renamed Silvio Pettirossi after an early Paraguayan aviator. A second, controversial international airport is being built close to the Brazilian border.

In marked contrast to the ox carts that rumble along the rural roads of Paraguay, any visitor to Asunción and other towns is soon aware of the unusual number of cars, some expensive, in the streets. Models include Mercedes-Benz coupes, Volvos, Jaguars, Argentine-built Renaults, and Brazilian Volkswagens. In Paraguayan they are called *Mau Mau* cars after a terrorist group in Kenya that always used to operate at night. Mau Mau cars are stolen, taken from Brazil and Argentina, almost always at night. They are driven over the border, with a small bribe to the customs official, and sold in Paraguay at much lower than the original cost.

COMMUNICATIONS

The first Asunción newspaper, *El Paraguayo Independiente*, was printed in 1845 at the instigation of Carlos Antonio López. Today several major newspapers published in the capital have circulations ranging from eight thousand to seventy-five thousand, of which the largest are *ABC Color, Ultima Hora,* and *El Diario.* English-language newspapers from Argentina and Brazil and daily papers from the United States can also be bought. A few periodicals are also published that cover political and family topics.

There are eleven commercial and one government radio station and four television channels, most of which are based in Asunción. Cable television is also available.

Particularly during the last years of the Stroessner regime, any

A bookstore in Encarnación

member of the media daring to express opposition to the government lived under threat of closure. The first to go, in 1984, was *ABC Color*, whose owner and director Aldo Zuccolillo was originally a Stroessner supporter and then an outspoken critic. In the seventeen years the paper was published before 1984 Zuccolillo was jailed twice, and members of his staff were imprisoned on thirty-two occasions. Between 1984 and 1989 other newspapers and periodicals were closed. Even radio stations did not escape. The most famous case was that of Radio Nanduti, whose director had been an opponent of Stroessner. It broadcast its own violent closure as it was happening, for all the world to hear. After the 1989 coup both *ABC Color* and Radio Nanduti were reinstated.

Several international news agencies are represented in Paraguay, and most towns can be dialed directly—nationally and internationally. There is also a good, widespread telex and telegram service.

The Bank of Brazil in Asunción

ROLE IN THE WORLD

Paraguay is a member of many international organizations.
Some, such as the Organization of American States, Latin
American Integration Association, and the Río de la Plata Basin
Organization, are concerned with matters directly related to the
continent and its development. Other organizations have
worldwide interests, for example, the World Health Organization
or the Food and Agricultural Organization, which are agencies of
the United Nations. On the commercial side Paraguay is a
member of various financial bodies, such as the World Bank and
the International Monetary Fund.

The republic enjoys representation in many overseas countries,
which is reciprocated with some thirty embassies or diplomatic
missions in Asunción, from other Latin American countries,
Europe, South Africa, the United States, and China, among others.
Paraguay's relationship with the United States is always of

paramount importance for both political and commercial reasons. Early in his presidency Stroessner received strong backing from the United States for his anti-Communist stand against Fidel Castro in Cuba. But later President Jimmy Carter drew the world's attention to the repression and human rights violations in the republic. By 1986 the Reagan administration, also critical of the Stroessner government, cut off military and economic aid. Financial and technical aid are as important as political backing to most of the Latin American countries, and the withdrawal at any time of aid from North America has serious repercussions. In Stroessner's case, it was certainly a contributory factor to his downfall.

It is equally important for Paraguay to remain on good terms with immediate neighbors, and peace has now been maintained in the region since the Chaco War in the 1930s. Political and economic unity is now the key phrase and if Mercosur, the economic bloc, can be made to work, it would be of great benefit to all the countries of the Río de la Plata.

THE FUTURE

In years to come, people may look back on the 1990s as a landmark in the history of Paraguay. At the outset of the decade, there are many good things on the horizon for the Republic.

The people put behind them the dictatorship of Alfredo Stroessner and survived their first elections in years. They look forward to real democratic elections in the future—real in the sense that opposition parties will have had time to prepare their candidates and policies. The first member of an opposition party has already been elected mayor of Asunción in council elections.

Young Paraguayan cowboys

The record-breaking Itaipú Dam was completed in 1991. Paraguay is on course to secure a firm economic base for the future. The country's own energy needs are less than one-half the output of one turbine, so there is ample surplus energy to sell or on which to base the development of its own industries. Paraguay is enjoying good relations with its neighbors and currently has greater and better access to the Atlantic than ever before.

There remains, however, one fundamental problem in Paraguay that must be addressed, and that is the allocation of land. The government can no longer turn a blind eye to the inequality of ownership, and a solution must be found so that the peasant families not only have their own land but are able to work it economically. If this can be resolved, then the people of the land of the rivers should enter the twenty-first century with great hopes for the future and with the freedom so long denied them.

Opposite page: Paraguay's forests must be protected before they all are destroyed. A view of downtown Asunción (inset)

MAP KEY

Acaray, *river*	D5	Fortin Ayacucho	A3	Puerto Pinasco	C4
Acaray, Represa de, *dam*	D5	Fortin Florida	B3	Puerto Presidente Stroessner	
Aguaray-Guazú, *river*	D3, D4	Fortin Garrapatal	B2	(renamed Ciudad del	
Aguaray-Guazú, *river*	C4, C5	Fortin Teniente Montania	C3	Este)	D5
Alberdi	E3	Fuerte Olimpo	B4	Puerto Sastre	C4
Alto Paraguay,		General Aquino	D4	Puerto Ybapobó	C4
department	A3, B3, C3	General Artigas	E4	Quiindy	D4
Alto Paraná,		General Eugenio A. Garay	B1	Quyquyó	E4
department	D5	Gran Chaco, *plain*	A3, B3, C3	Riacho Alegre, *river*	B3
Alto Paraná, *river*	E5	Guairá, *department*	D4, D5	Riacho González, *river*	C3
Amambay, *department*	C4, C5	Guairá, Salto del, *waterfall*	D5	Riacho Mosquito, *river*	C3
Amambay, Cordillera de,		Hernandarias	D5	Riacho San Carlos, *river*	C3, C4
mountains	C5	Hohenau	E5	Rosario	D4
Antequera	D4	Horqueta	C4	Salado, *river*	D4
Apa, *river*	C4	Humanitá	E3	Salto del Guairá	D5
Aquidabán, *river*	C4	Itacurubi del Rosario	D4	San Bernardino	D4
Arroyos y Esteros	D4	Itaipú, Represa de, *dam*	D5	San Carlos	C4
Asunción	D4	Itapúa, *department*	E4, E5	San Estanislao	D4
Belén	C4	Itaquyry	D5	San Ignacio	E4
Boquerón,		Iturbe	E4	San Joaquin	D4
department	C1, C2, C3	Jejui-Guazú *river*	D5	San José	D4
Caacupé	D4	Jesús	E5	San Juan Bautista	E4
Caaguazú	D4	La Colmena	D4	San Juan Nepomuceno	E5
Caaguazú, Cordillera de,		La Esmeralda	C1	San Lázaro	C4
mountains	D4, D5	Lambaré	D4	San Miguel	E4
Caaguazú, *department*	D4, D5	Lima	C4	San Pedro	D4
Caapucú	E4	Loreto	C4	San Pedro, *department*	C4, D4
Caazapá	E4	Mariscal Estigarribia	C2	San Pedro del Paraná	E4
Caazapá,		Mayor Pablo Lagerenza	A2	San Rafael, Cerro, *mountain*	E5
department	E4, E5	Mbaracayú, Cordillera de,		San Rafael, Cordillera de,	
Canendiyú,		*mountains*	C5, D5	*mountains*	E5
department	C5, D4, D5	Mbuyapey	E4	Santa Rosa	B2
Capiibary, *river*	D4	Misiones, *department*	E4	Santa Rosa	E4
Capitán Bado	C5	Monday, *river*	D5	Santiago	E4
Capitán Meza	E5	Montelindo, *river*	C2, C3	Santisima Trinidad	D4
Caraguatay	D4	Nacunday	E5	Sapucai	D4
Carapá, *river*	D5	Neembucú, *department*	E3, E4	Sieté Puntas, *river*	C3, C4
Carapeguá	D4	Negro, *river*	D3, D4	Tacuati	C4
Carayaó	D4	Nueva Asunción,		Tavai	E5
Central, *department*	D4	*department*	B1, B2, B3	Tebicuary, *river*	E3, E4, E5
Chaco,		Nueva Germania	C4	Tebicuary-mi, *river*	E4
department	A2, A3, B2, B3	Paraguari	D4	Timane, *river*	B2, B3
Chaco Boreal, *plain*	A2, A3, B2	Paraguari, *department*	D4, E4	Unión	D4
Concepción	C4	Paraguay, *river*	B3, B4, C4, D4	Verde, *river*	C2, C3, C4
Concepción, *department*	C4	Pedro Juan Caballero	C5	Villa Florida	E4
Confuso, *river*	D3	Pilar	E3	Villa Hayes	D4
Corá, Cerro, *hill*	C4	Pilcomayo, *river*	C2, D3	Villarrica	D4
Cordillera, *department*	D4	Piribebuy	D4	Yacyretá, Isla, *island*	E4
Coronel Bogado	E4	Pozo Colorado	C3	Yacyretá-Apipé, Represa de,	
Coronel Oviedo	D4	Presidente Hayes,		*dam*	E4
Curuguaty	D5	*department*	C3, C4, D3, D4	Yegros	E4
Doctor Cecilio Báez	D4	Puerto Adela	D5	Ygatimi	D5
Doctor Pedro P. Peña	C1	Puerto Bahia Negra	B3	Ygauzú, *river*	D5
Domingo M. Irala	D5	Puerto Casado	C4	Ypané, *river*	C4
Emboscada	D4	Puerto Fonciere	C4	Ypé Jhú	C5
Encarnación	E5	Puerto Guarani	B4	Ypoá, Lago, *lake*	D4, E4
Fernando de la Mora	D4	Puerto Leda	B4	Ytambey, *river*	D5
Filadelfia	C2	Puerto Mihanovich	B4	Yuty	E4

112

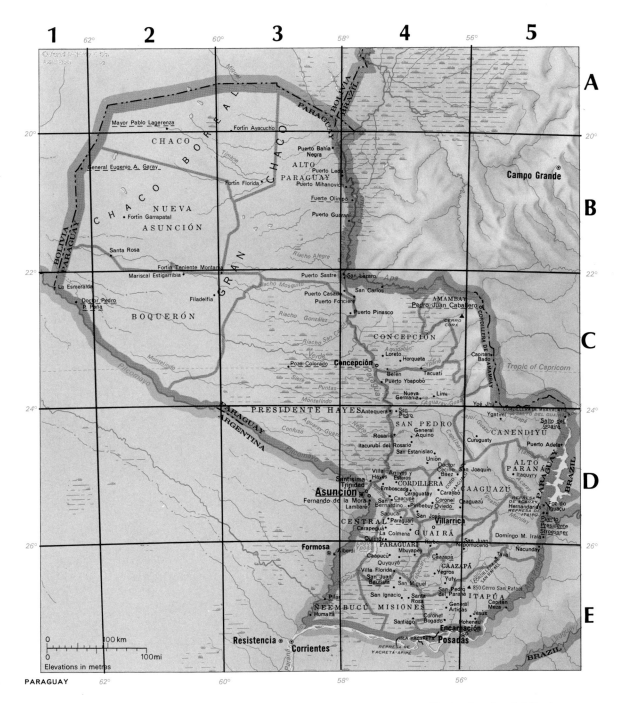

A

20°

Mayor Pablo Lagerenza

CHACO   BOREAL

Fortín Ayacucho

Puerto Bahía Negra

ALTO PARAGUAY

Puerto Leda

Puerto Mihanovich

Campo Grande

General Eugenio A. Garay

Fortín Florida

BOLIVIA PARAGUAY
BRAZIL

B

CHACO

NUEVA ASUNCIÓN

Fortín Garrapatal

Fuerte Olimpo

Puerto Guaraní

Riacho Alegre

Santa Rosa

BOLIVIA PARAGUAY

22°

Fortín Teniente Montanía

Mariscal Estigarribia

Puerto Sastre

Puerto Casado

San Lázaro

Apa

San Carlos

AMAMBAY

Pedro Juan Caballero

La Esmeralda

GRAN   CHACO

Filadelfia

Riacho Mosquito

Puerto Fonciere

Puerto Pinasco

CERRO CORÁ

CORDILLERA DE AMAMBAY

C

Doctor Pedro P. Peña

BOQUERÓN

Riacho González

Riacho San Carlos

Verde

CONCEPCIÓN

Aguidabán

Loreto

Horqueta

Capitán Bado

Tropic of Capricorn

Montelindo

Picomayo

Pozo Colorado

Concepción

Belén

Tacuatí

Puerto Ybapobó

Lima

Siete Puntas

Nueva Germania

Ypé Jhú

Montelindo

CORDILLERA DE MBARACAYÚ
SALTO DEL GUAIRÁ

24°

PRESIDENTE HAYES

Antequera

San Pedro

Ygatimí

Salto del Guairá

PARAGUAY ARGENTINA

Confuso

Picomayo

Aguaray-Guazú

Negro

SAN PEDRO

General Aquino

Curuguaty

CANENDIYÚ

Puerto Adela

Itacurubí del Rosario

Rosario

San Estanislao

Unión

Doctor Cecilio Báez

San Joaquín

ALTO PARANÁ

BRAZIL

D

Santísima Trinidad

Villa Hayes

Arroyos y Esteros

CORDILLERA

Caaguazú

Itaquyry

Foz do Iguaçu

Asunción

Emboscada

Paraguatí

Carayaó

Caaguazú

REPRESA DE ACARAY

Puerto Presidente Stroessner

Fernando de la Mora

Lambaré

San Bernardino

Caacupé

Piribebuy

Coronel Oviedo

REPRESA DE ITAIPU

Monday

Sapucaí

San José

Villarrica

Domingo M. Irala

CENTRAL

Paraguarí

GUAIRÁ

Carapeguá

La Colmena

San Juan Nepomuceno

Ñacunday

26°

Quiindy

PARAGUARÍ

Formosa

Alberdi

Caapucú

Mbuyapey

Caazapá

Tavaí

CORDILLERA DE SAN RAFAEL

Quyquyó

CAAZAPÁ

Villa Florida

Yegros

Yuty

San Juan Bautista

San Miguel

850 Cerro San Rafael

Pilar

San Ignacio

Santa Rosa

San Pedro del Paraná

ITAPÚA

Capitán Meza

NEEMBUCÚ

MISIONES

General Artigas

Jesús

E

Humaitá

Santiago

Coronel Bogado

Hohenau

Encarnación

Resistencia

Corrientes

Paraná

ISLA YACYRETÁ

REPRESA DE YACYRETÁ-APIPÉ

Posadas

BRAZIL

0   100 km
0   100 mi
Elevations in metres

Map from Encyclopedia Britannica
© 1993 by Rand McNally, R.L. 93-S-107

MINI-FACTS AT A GLANCE

GENERAL INFORMATION

Official Name: República del Paraguay (Republic of Paraguay)

Capital: Asunción

Government: Paraguay is a republic with two legislative houses. The president is the head of the state and government and is elected for a five-year term. The president must be a Roman Catholic and over forty years old. The president appoints five members of the Supreme Court, and also appoints an advisory board called the Council of State. Legislative power is vested in the National Congress made up of the Senate with 36 members and a Chamber of Deputies with 72 members. The Colorado party has been in political power since 1948. Administratively the country is divided into two regions, and 19 departments.

Religion: Roman Catholicism is the official religion followed by almost 96 percent of the population. There is a great respect for local patron saints and annual festivities are held in their honor.

Ethnic Composition: The largest ethnic group is mestizo (Spanish-Indian), forming some 91 percent of the total population; followed by Indians, 3 percent; Germans, 2 percent; and others, 4 percent. A small number of blacks live on the border with Brazil. Native Indians number about forty thousand. The Guaraní are the largest group of Indians; others are the Caingang and the Guayakí. The Maca Indian tribe lives independently on an island close to Asunción. There are small colonies of people of European origin.

Language: Spanish is the official language. The majority of the mestizos are bilingual, speaking both Spanish and Guaraní.

National Flag: The flag has three horizontal stripes, red, white, and blue. The national emblem appears in the center of the white stripe on the front and the treasury seal appears on the back; the seal depicts a lion guarding a staff bearing a red cap of liberty. The present flag has been in use since 1842.

National Emblem: It consists of a red and gold five-pointed star (called May Star) with golden rays, and is surrounded by palm and olive branches tied together at the base with ribbons in the national colors. The May Star stands for independence from Spain. The name Republica del Paraguay appears in a semicircle in the middle.

National Anthem: "Paraguayos, república o muerte!" ("Paraguayans, Republic or Death!")

Money: Paraguayan guaraní (G) of 100 centimos is the official currency. In May 1993 1 US$ was equal to G 1,715.

Membership in International Organizations: International Monetary Fund (IMF), Latin American Integration Association, Organization of American States (OAS), Río de la Plata Basin Organization, United Nations (UN), World Bank, and World Health Organization (WHO)

Weights and Measures: The metric system is in force.

Population: 1991 population 4,397,000; population density 28 persons per sq. mi. (11 persons per sq km); 46 percent urban and 54 percent rural.

Cities:

Asunción 607,700
San Lorenzo . . . . 123,737 (1985 census)
Ciudad del Este
    (formerly Puerto Presidente Stroessner) 110,584
Concepción . . . . 62,577 (1985 census)
Encarnación 44,064

(Unless noted, population is based on the 1990 census.)

GEOGRAPHY

Area: 157,048 sq. mi. (406,755 sq km); one of the smallest countries in South America

Border: 2,358 mi. (3,794 km). Borders are shared with Brazil in the north and northeast, with Argentina in the south, west, and southeast, and with Bolivia in the north and northwest. Rivers make up four-fifths of Paraguay's border.

Coastline: None; it is a landlocked country.

Land: Río Paraguay, flowing through Paraguay for 700 mi. (1,127 km), divides the country into two sharply contrasting regions—sparsely populated Chaco region in the west and Paraguay proper—a fertile and cultivated plateau in the east. The Chaco is part of the largest Gran Chaco that extends into Argentina, Bolivia, and Brazil. Major mountain ranges include Cordillera de Amambay and Cordillera de Mbaracayú in the northeast, and the Cordillera de Caaguazú in the southwest. Chaco is a level, almost featureless land; its southern parts are swampy while the northern part is hotter, with scrub vegetation.

Highest Point: San Rafael Peak at 2,789 ft. (850 m)

Lowest Point: 180 ft. (55 m) at the meeting point of the Paraguay and Paraná rivers

Rivers: Rivers are Paraguay's richest natural resource. The river network connects Paraguay with the Río de la Plata estuary in Argentina, giving Paraguay access to the Atlantic Ocean. The three major rivers are the Paraguay, the Paraná, and the Pilcomayo; these are the transportation arteries of this landlocked nation. The Friendship Bridge over the Río Paraná links Paraguay with Brazil. The Itaipú hydroelectric dam on Brazil-Paraguay border has shown tremendous impact on Paraguay's economy; it is the world's largest hydroelectric dam. Most of Paraguay's energy needs are satisfied by hydroelectricity. The largest lake is the Ypoa. Lake Ypacaraí near Asunción is only 10 ft. (3 m) deep, and is a popular vacation center.

Forests: Almost one-half of the country is under forests, and another 35 percent is under meadows and pastures. Since the 1940s over 12 million acres (4,856,280 hectares) of forest have been lost and the destruction is continuing. As a measure of conservation a law was enacted that bans the export of logs to Brazil. Hardwood trees are more abundant in the east while palm, quebracho, ceiba, and medicinal herbs and shrubs are common in the west. The lapacho tree, which flowers abundantly in July and August, is the national tree. Yerba maté, a holly tree, grows wild in the northeast.

Wildlife: Crocodiles were once in abundance in Paraguay. Peccaries (similar to wild pigs), jaguars, monkeys, foxes, brown wolves, armadillos, brocket deer, rabbit-sized agoutis, butterflies, and pacas are common in the forests. Water boas and large semiaquatic rodents, capybaras, are found in swampy areas. The rhea is the largest (5 ft.; 1.5 m) bird found in Paraguay, Other birds include hummingbirds, herons, egrets, wood storks, maguari storks, toucans, parrots, parakeets, macaws, ovenbirds, and firewood gatherers.

Climate: Since Paraguay lies south of the equator, the winter months are June and July. Two-thirds of the country lies within the temperate climate zone. The subtropical climate has few extremes of temperature. Frost can occur in wintertime, but snow is unknown. Temperatures in Asunción average 65° F. (18.3° C) in July and 84° F. (28.8° C) in January. Rainfall is greatest in the north and east and gradually decreases. Occasionally heavy rains cause serious flooding of the major rivers.

Greatest Distance: North to South: 575 mi. (925 km)
East to West: 410 mi. (660 km)

ECONOMY AND INDUSTRY

Agriculture: Some one-fifth of the total land is suitable for intensive cultivation, and about 40 percent of the working population is involved in agriculture. Agriculture accounts for some 90 percent of the total exports. Chief agricultural products are cassava, sugarcane, soybeans, corn, wheat, beans, potatoes, tung oil, bananas, oranges, peanuts, cotton, melons, tomatoes, lettuce, and sweet potatoes.

The slash-and-burn method of agriculture is still practiced in some remote areas. Paraguay has a vast disparity in land holdings—some 80 percent of land is held by 1 percent of landowners. Typically a family may farm one or two acres of land on which they have their houses, a small barn, and a pen for pigs and chickens. Many small farms have trees for oranges, limes, and holly (yerba maté). Small farmers rely on oxen to plough the fields and to transport produce to and from market. Floods and drought frequently affect crop production.

Cattle raising is mainly concentrated in the Chaco. Dairy cattle is the main industry of Mennonites—a religious sect originally from Germany—producing milk, yogurt, butter, and cheese. A variety of fish is found in rivers, lagoons, and coastal waters: dorado, catfish, piranha, and ray are the most common.

Mining: Paraguay has small deposits of limestone, uranium, malachite, azurite, marble, salt, bauxite, iron ore, manganese, copper, kaolin, and gypsum. There has been much oil exploration but nothing substantial has been found.

Manufacturing: This sector employs some 15 percent of the total work force. Meat and timber processing, cement, sugar, tung oil, processing of hides and coconut, cotton ginning, textiles, beverages, and cigarettes are the main manufacturing items. Most of the industries are based in Asunción. A steel mill provides steel goods for the construction industry. There is also a small shipbuilding industry.

Transportation: Traditionally the route to the sea of this landlocked country has been through its rivers. Asunción is the largest port with modern facilities. In the early 1990s there were about 15,960 mi. (25,684 km) of roads out of which roughly 10 percent are paved. The all-weather Trans-Chaco Highway connects Filadelfia with Asunción. Three bridges connecting Paraguay with Brazil and Argentina have facilitated road transport. The railway network is poor with only 270 mi. (435 km) of railway lines. The only major railway, both for freight and passengers, connects Asunción with Encarnación; a steam locomotive railway line connects Asunción with Lake Ypacaraí, a tourist place. Líneas Aéreas Paraguayas is the national airline; Asunción is the largest international airport.

Communication: Six daily newpapers, including *ABC Color, Ultima Hora,* and *El Diario,* serve the country. There are several commercial and one government radio stations and television channels. In the early 1990s, there were some 6 people per radio receiver, 12 people per television set, and some 35 people per telephone. A good, widespread telex and telegram service connects most of the towns and cities. Both national and international calls can be dialed directly.

Trade: Chief imports are machinery and transport equipment, fuels and lubricants, tobacco and beverages, chemicals and pharmaceuticals, and iron and steel products. Major import sources are Brazil, Japan, Argentina, United States, Germany, and Algeria. Principal export items are cotton and fibers, soybeans, processed meats, timber, perfume oils, coffee, and vegetable oils. Major export destinations are Brazil, the Netherlands, Argentina, Switzerland, Germany, United

States, and Italy. Paraguay has duty-free facilities at the Brazilian port of Paranaguá for freight handling for export.

EVERYDAY LIFE

Health: Most prevalent health problems include diseases of the circulatory and respiratory systems, infectious and parasitic diseases, and cancers. Insect-borne disease claims many lives every year. Poor water supplies are another health hazard; less than half of the population has access to safe water.

Education: Some 80.5 percent of the population can read and write. By law, children are required to attend school for six years starting at age seven; secondary schools lasts for another six years. Education facilities are easily available in cities and towns, but in rural areas schools are very few and are not well equipped. Also, many rural children drop out of school to help their families farm the land. The state and church run the majority of the schools, but there are some private schools. The medium of instruction is both Spanish and Guaraní. There are some vocational schools for technical or agricultural training. Higher education is limited to the state-run National University of Asunción, and the Catholic University with five campuses. Some wealthy students go overseas to attend universities.

Holidays:

> New Year's Day, January 1
> San Blas Day, February 3
> Heroes' Day, March 1
> Labor Day, May 1
> National Day (Independence Day), May 14 and 15
> Peace of Chaco Day, June 12
> Constitution Day, August 25
> Columbus Day, October 12
> Christmas, December 25

Culture: Asunción has the country's principal libraries and museums, including the National Museum and Archives, the National Museum of Fine Arts and Antiquities, and the Museum of Modern Art. The Government Palace, also known as the López Palace, in Asunción is built in the style of the Louvre in Paris. Other points of interest in the capital city include the Legislative Palace, the Cathedral, Plaza de los Héroes, Plaza Uruguay, and House of Independence (a museum with colonial relics). The Franciscan church at Yaguarón is outstanding in its architecture and beautiful wood carvings; it is considered to be one of the finest Indian baroque churches in Spanish America. The Guaraní produce beautifully woven carpets, boats, and illuminated manuscripts.

Handicrafts: The Nanduti lace is perhaps the most famous and beautiful handicraft of Paraguay. It is woven from a piece of cloth stretched onto a wooden frame using any of a hundred or so different patterns. It is used for place mats, collars and cuffs, scarves or veils, and sometimes wedding dresses. Cotton spinning and weaving are other traditional handicrafts.

Housing: In rural areas houses are built of adobe, brick, and concrete blocks or timber. Roofing may be of tiles, palm thatch, or corrugated iron. Sometimes cooking is done on an open fire; bread is baked in a dome-shaped mud oven outside the home. Some poor squatters live near large urban areas in shacks with no water or light. In cities and towns Spanish-style large houses with running water and electricity are becoming common. The majority of the city houses have red tile roofs and iron grillwork covering the windows. There are many luxury mansions with fine landscaped gardens. A broad range of apartments and single or two-story houses are common in the suburbs.

Dress: Many rural women wear a long, full skirt and a simple blouse. They wear a shawl, *rebozo*, that covers the upper body. Men generally wear loose trousers called *bombachas* with a shirt. They wear a poncho over the shirt.

Food: Many different type of soups are prepared with meat, vegetables, and cheese. *Sopa paraguaya*, made of ground maize and cheese, is the national dish. *Chipa soo* is a maize bread filled with meat. *Asados* are large-scale barbecues. Some fast food shops in Asunción sell chicken and hamburgers. The Paraguayan diet also contains a good proportion of fish; *surubi* or catfish is salted and preserved. *Yerba maté* is a refreshing tea that is made from the leaves of a native plant. Drinking yerba maté is a way of life for Paraguayans. Another popular drink, *mosto*, is chilled sugarcane juice.

Sports and Recreation: The most popular sport is soccer. Virtually every town or village has a local soccer team. Basketball, tennis, golf, and rugby are enjoyed too. Large cities have motorboat, swimming, and rowing clubs. Paraguayans are traditionally skilled horsemen and rodeos are greatly enjoyed as family outings.
   Music and dance have always been important. Indians have a variety of flutes made from wood and cane. The guitar and harp are Paraguay's national instruments. Dances include the polka, waltz, galop, and folk dances including the "bottle dance," the Santa Fé, and the Pericón.

Social Welfare: The National Indian Institute (INDI) is responsible for the welfare and well-being of Paraguay's indigenous Indians. Some one-fifth of the total expenditure of the central government is spent on social security and welfare. Benefits include free medical care, maternity care, sickness, accident, and retirement benefits.

IMPORTANT DATES

1516—The first recorded Spanish expedition, led by Juan Díaz de Solis, enters the Río de la Plata estuary

1526—Sebastian Cabot arrives off the Brazilian coast

1537—The colony of Nuestra Señora de la Asunción is established; later it becomes the capital city of Paraguay

1565—The first Jesuit bishop arrives in Asunción

1580—Buenos Aires is finally and successfully refounded

1609—The first Jesuit mission is established

1617—The Spanish crown separates Buenos Aires from the Colony of Paraguay

1721—Criollo uprising against Spanish authority

1767—Jesuit missionaries are expelled from Paraguay and from all the Spanish colonies in South America

1772—The whitewashed *Casa de la Independencia* is built

1776—Paraguay province is made part of the Viceroyalty of La Plata based in Buenos Aires

1808—Napoleon Bonaparte invades Spain

1810—The Spanish Viceroy of Buenos Aires is deposed

1811—Argentina recognizes the independence of Paraguay

1813—Paraguay formally declares independence

1814—Dr. José Gaspar Rodríguez de Francia is declared supreme dictator of Paraguay

1816—Francia is declared dictator for life

1820—Francia discovers a conspiracy to depose him; he orders the arrest and torture of hundreds of suspects

1842—Slavery is abolished in Paraguay by President Carlos Antonio López

1844—A congress is convened; it ratifies the constitution and elects López as the first president

1845—The first newspaper *El Paraguayo Independiente* is printed; a telegraph line is started

1855—Brazil puts a major naval expedition on the Río Paraná

1861 — Carlos Antonio López Railway Station is built

1864 — Brazil invades Uruguay

1865-70 — War of the Triple Alliance; Paraguayan fleet is virtually destroyed; more than 275,000 killed in War of the Triple Alliance

1876 — Paraguay is freed from Argentine and Brazilian occupation

1884 — War between Bolivia and Chile

1904 — The Liberal party forms a government

1904-1912 — Ten different presidents rule in Paraguay

1910 — The National Academy of Fine Arts is established

1911 — Paraguay has four different presidents in one year

1920s — Mennonites begin colonies

1932-38 — Chaco War, between Paraguay and Bolivia

1932 — Bolivian forces attack a Paraguayan fort

1938 — Peace treaty is signed between Bolivia and Paraguay

1953 — Presidential elections are won by Dr. Federico Chávez

1954 — The Colorado party and the military join to install General Alfredo Stroessner president; he serves until 1989

1973 — Work on Itaipú Dam begins

1982 — The first stage of the Itaipú hydroelectric dam is completed

1983 — Heavy rains cause flooding of Río Paraguay

1984 — *ABC Color* newspaper is closed because of government criticism (is reinstated after 1989 coup)

1986 — U.S. government cuts off economic and military aid to the Stroessner government

1987 — *El Pueblo* newspaper is closed for criticism of the government

1989 — Dictatorship is ended with the ouster of President Stroessner; *ABC Color* and *El Pueblo* newspapers reopen

1990 — Armed forces are prohibited from joining political parties

1991 — The 18th and last turbine is placed at Itaipú Dam

1992 — Paraguay, Brazil, Argentina, and Uruguay create Mercosur, a four-country, free-trade bloc

1993 — Juan Carlos Wasmosy of the Colorado party is elected president

IMPORTANT PEOPLE

Pablo Alborno (1877-1958), artist; introduced impressionism into Paraguay; helped establish the National Academy of Fine Arts

Hernando Arias de Saavedra (c.1561-c.1634), also known as Hernandarias, the first governor of the Spanish Colony of Paraguay

Eusebio Ayala (1875-1942), an intellectual and authority on political economy and international law; Paraguayan leader and provisional president 1921-23 and president 1932-36

Cecilio Báez (1862-1941), an intellectual; president of Paraguay from 1907 to 1908; founder of the Liberal party

General Manuel Belgrano (1770-1820), Argentine military leader

Jaime Bestard (1892-   ), impressionist artist; his favorite subjects were local fiestas, cockfights, and landscapes

Joseph Bonaparte (1768-1844), brother of Napoleon Bonaparte; installed king of Spain by Napoleon in 1808

Napoleon Bonaparte (1769-1821), also known as Napoleon I, French emperor from 1805 to 1815

Sebastian Cabot (1476?-1557), navigator and mapmaker; arrived off the Brazilian coast in 1526

Dr. Federico Chávez (1882-   ), leader of the Colorado party, elected provincial president in 1949 and president in 1953

Juan Díaz de Solís (1470?-1516), Spanish navigator, led the first recorded Spanish expedition in the Río de la Plata estuary

Manuel Dominguez (1869-1935), writer

José Felix Estigarribia (1888-1940), general, hero of the Chaco War; president from 1939 to 1940; introduced a new constitution

Dr. José Gaspar Rodríguez de Francia. *See entry* under Rodríguez

Colonel Rafael Franco (1897-   ), became president of Paraguay in 1936 after a military coup

Aleixo García (1471-1535), one of the first white men to sail up the Río Paraguay; attacked the Incas with the help of the Guaraní

Gigno García, harpist

W. Barbrooke Grubb, Anglican missionary; legal representative of the government in the Chaco region for 18 years; helped exploit Indian lands

Julián de la Herrería, artist, best known for his sympathetic paintings of Indians

Carlos Antonio López (1792-1862), lawyer and leader after Francia; first president of Paraguay from 1844 to 1862; opened Paraguay's borders to the outside world

Francisco Solano López (1826-1870), also called Marshal López; son of Carlos Antonio López; succeeded as president (1862-70) after death of his father

Eliza Lynch (1835-86), an Irish woman; companion of Marshal López and mother of his four children

Pedro de Mendoza (1487-1537), Spanish soldier and explorer, who plundered the Inca lands for gold and silver; sailed up Río de la Plata and founded the first colony of Buenos Aires in 1536

Higinio Morínigo (1508-60), Chaco War hero; president of Paraguay in the 1940s

Felix Pérez Cardoso, harpist

Augusto Roa Bastos (1917-   ), writer

Hugo Rodríguez Alcala (1917-   ), writer

Dr. José Gaspar Rodríguez de Francia (1766-1840), dictator called "El Supremo"; a civilian lawyer; negotiated a treaty with Argentina that recognized Paraguay's independence

Juan Manuel de Rosas (1793-1877), dictator of Argentina; closed Río de la Plata to Paraguayan ships and trade

Juan de Salazar, one of the commanders of Mendoza; he chose the site of Asunción

General Alfredo Stroessner (1912-   ), dictator of Paraguay from 1954 to 1989; became commander-in-chief of the armed forces in 1951; turned Asunción into a modern capital

Juan Carlos Wasmosy (1939-   ), member of the Colorado party elected to a 5-year term as president in 1993

Fulgencio Yegros (1770-1821), led the Paraguay junta that governed the republic after independence; responsible for deposing the last Spanish governor in Paraguay; an associate of Francia

Aldo Zuccolillo, owner and director of *ABC Color* newspaper

INDEX

Page numbers that appear in boldface type indicate illustrations

About the Author

Newly graduated with a degree in history from the University of Wales, Marion Morrison first traveled to South America in 1962 with a British volunteer program to work among Aymara Indians living near Lake Titicaca. In Bolivia she met her husband, British filmmaker and writer, Tony Morrison. In the last twenty-five years the Morrisons, who make their home in England, have visited almost every country of South and Central America, making television documentary films, photographing, and researching—sometimes accompanied by their children, Kimball and Rebecca.

Marion Morrison has written about South American countries for Macmillan's Let's Visit series, and for Wayland Publishers' Peoples, How They Lived and Life and Times series. Mrs. Morrison also has written *Bolivia, Colombia, Uruguay,* and *Venezuela* in the Enchantment of the World series. Resulting from their travels, the Morrisons have created their South American Picture Library that contains more than seventy-five thousand pictures of the continent.